FOUNDATIONS
OF
DEMOCRACY:

*Authority, Privacy,
Responsibility, and Justice*

Level V – Middle School and Above

Teacher's Guide

Law in a Free Society Series

Center for Civic Education

5146 Douglas Fir Road • Calabasas, CA 91302 • (818) 591-9321

Cover: Construction of the Treasury Building, September 16, 1861 (Library of Congress Photo)
Cover Design: Richard Stein

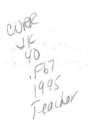

The first edition of this text was developed with the support of a grant from the National Endowment for the Humanities.

This new and revised edition has been prepared under Grant #85-JS-CX-0009 from the Office of Juvenile Justice and Delinquency Prevention, Office of Justice Programs, U.S. Department of Justice.

Points of view or opinions in this document are those of the author and do not necessarily represent the official position or policies of the U.S. Department of Justice.

ISBN 0-89818-151-8

EXECUTIVE DIRECTOR
Charles N. Quigley

CURRICULUM DEVELOPERS
Margaret S. Branson
Beth E. Farnbach
Jack N. Hoar
Joseph S. Jackson
Charles N. Quigley

PRINCIPAL AUTHOR
Kenneth Rodriguez

PRODUCTION DIRECTOR
Patricia Mathwig

EDITORS
Michelle L. Forner
Theresa M. Richard

TYPESETTER
Valerie Milianni

The Center for Civic Education thanks the following writers for their contributions to the first edition of these texts: Mara Braverman, Marshall Croddy, Edward Hirsch, and Jerold A. Rosen.

CONSULTANTS

William Landau
Associate Professor of English
Los Angeles Pierce College

Herbert Morris
Professor of Law and Philosophy
University of California, Los Angeles

Richard P. Longaker
Vice-President of Academic Affairs Emeritus
The Johns Hopkins University

Duane E. Smith
Professor Emeritus, Political Science
University of California, Los Angeles

Dear Educator:

From the inception of the public school system in America, educational institutions have played a major role in preparing young people for citizenship. Schools today, as in the infancy of our republic, must serve to nurture and sustain civic competence, civic responsibility, and a reasoned commitment to our most fundamental principles and values. For as thinkers like Thomas Jefferson and John Adams recognized, a constitutional democracy, more than any other type of government, depends upon an informed and responsible citizenry.

The *Foundations of Democracy* curriculum is designed to assist schools in fulfilling this critical role. Organized around the concepts of authority, privacy, responsibility, and justice, the curriculum challenges students to think for themselves, to develop reasoned positions, and to articulate and defend their views. Substantive instruction in areas fundamental to our scheme of ordered liberty is conveyed through interactive teaching strategies that engage students' interest and foster civic participation skills. With your guidance, *Foundations of Democracy* will help prepare your students to be active and effective citizens in our constitutional democracy.

Sincerely,

Charles N. Quigley
Executive Director
Center for Civic Education

"Liberty without learning is always in peril and learning without liberty is always in vain."
John Fitzgerald Kennedy

Contents

Effective Citizenship Education Programs' Characteristics

Effective citizenship education programs are distinguished by at least four characteristics:

- **Extensive interaction among students.** Teaching strategies that foster interactive and cooperative learning among students are keys to development of civic participation skills and responsible citizenship. Examples of these teaching strategies are small group work, simulations, role-play activities, and moot courts.

- **Realistic content that includes balanced treatment of issues.** Realistic and fair treatment of issues is an essential component of effective citizenship education. So is critical thinking about all sides to controversies. If our legal and political systems are presented as flawless or infallible, students will doubt the credibility of the teacher and the practicality of the content. By contrast, if only cases in which the system has failed are presented, students will be less likely to view the system as a positive means for maintaining social order and justice. A balance should be sought between respect for the legal and political system and constructive criticism about its application in specific cases.

- **Use of community resource persons in the classroom.** Interaction with a variety of adult role models who work within our legal and political system adds credibility and reality to the curriculum and is a powerful influence on development of positive attitudes toward the legal and political system. Appropriate use of resource persons in the classroom (e.g., lawyers, judges, police officers, legislators, etc.) is strongly associated with increased student interest in issues related to effective citizenship and with positive responses to teachers and the school.

- **Strong support for citizenship education by the principal and other important school administrators.** A key to successful implementation of citizenship education in the schools is strong support by administrators, especially the school principal. Supportive administrators can aid citizenship education by organizing opportunities for peer support, rewarding teachers for outstanding work, helping teachers explain and justify the program to people in the community outside the school, and providing opportunities for staff development in knowledge and skills needed to carry out citizenship education programs. In addition, positive attitudes about citizenship education on the part of teachers and their colleagues are very important to successful implementation.

Successful citizenship programs involve students actively in the learning process in ways that reflect a high regard for each person. Reflection, deliberation, and discourse are valued and practiced systematically. The development of knowledge and character are pursued in concert as equally important elements of responsible citizenship in our constitutional democracy. Every attempt has been made to incorporate these essential characteristics in the *Foundations of Democracy* curriculum.

Foundations of Democracy
Curriculum Rationale

A fundamental hypothesis of the *Foundations of Democracy* curriculum is that education can increase a person's capacity and inclination to act knowledgeably, effectively, and responsibly. It follows that the role of educational institutions must be to help students increase their capacity to make intelligent choices for themselves—to learn *how* to think, rather than *what* to think. The alternative, indoctrination, is improper for educational institutions in a free society.

The Center for Civic Education was founded on the belief that the learning experiences provided by a curriculum based on this philosophy result in significant progress towards students' development of a rational and profound commitment to those principles, processes, and values that are essential to the preservation and improvement of our free society.

Curriculum Goals

The *Foundations of Democracy* curriculum is designed to

- promote an increased understanding of the institutions of our constitutional democracy and the fundamental principles and values upon which they were founded

- develop the skills needed by young people to become effective and responsible citizens

- increase understanding and willingness to use democratic processes when making decisions and managing conflict, both in public and private life

In studying *Foundations of Democracy*, students develop the ability to identify issues that require social action. They are encouraged through informed inquiry to make a personal commitment to accept the responsibilities associated with the rights we enjoy as citizens—responsibilities essential to the continued existence of a society based on the ideals of justice, equality, freedom, and human rights.

Curriculum Organization

This is not a conventional text which focuses on facts, dates, people, and events. Rather, *Foundations of Democracy* is about ideas, values, and principles fundamental to understanding our constitutional democracy. The curriculum is organized around four concepts, **authority**, **privacy**, **responsibility**, and **justice**, which form part of the common core of civic values and concepts that are fundamental to the theory and practice of democratic citizenship in the United States. These concepts are not discrete or mutually exclusive; some often conflict with others. They are subject to many different interpretations, as all really important ideas are.

Foundations of Democracy may be taught in its entirety, or the teacher may select specific concepts as they relate to general curriculum goals and learning outcomes in a school or district. The concepts need not be taught in any particular order. If you select a single lesson, however, you are only addressing the objectives of that specific lesson and not the goals of a unit or concept.

Each of the four concepts in this curriculum is organized into four units of study, each designed to answer a fundamental question about the nature and application of that concept. Below is a brief description of the four units of study within each concept.

Unit One: What Is Authority? Students learn the relationship between power and authority, investigate the various sources of authority, and gain a perspective on authority by studying situations in which there is an absence of authority or a misuse of authority. They then examine ways to deal with such situations wisely and effectively.

Unit Two: How Can We Evaluate Rules and Laws, and Candidates for Positions of Authority? Students acquire the knowledge and skills to make informed and reasoned decisions about matters relating to rules and people in authority.

Unit Three: What Are the Benefits and Costs of Using Authority? Students learn that every exercise of authority carries with it certain advantages and disadvantages for individuals and for society as a whole. It is necessary to understand the benefits and costs of authority in order to make intelligent decisions about what the scope and limits of authority should be.

Unit Four: What Should Be the Scope and Limits of Authority? This unit prepares students to make decisions about the powers and the limits which ought to be assigned to a particular position of authority so that the use of authority can be effective but not oppressive.

Authority

Unit One: What Is the Importance of Privacy? This unit helps students to define privacy and to understand its importance, to identify and describe common objects of privacy in different situations, and to discriminate between situations in which privacy does and does not exist.

Unit Two: What Factors Explain Differences in Privacy Behavior? This unit helps students understand the factors or elements that explain differences in the privacy behavior of individuals. Students learn that although privacy exists in all cultures there are often differences in the privacy behavior of individuals within a culture and between different cultures.

Privacy

Unit Three: What Are Some Benefits and Costs of Privacy? This unit helps students understand that every time we maintain privacy there are certain consequences. Some consequences are advantages, some are disadvantages. Students also learn that different individuals may have different opinions about whether the right to privacy should be protected in a particular situation.

Unit Four: What Should Be the Scope and Limits of Privacy? This unit helps students understand that some of the most important issues we face as citizens involve questions about the scope and limits of privacy: What kinds of things will we allow people to keep private? When will we require privacy to give way to other values?

Responsibility

Unit One: What Is the Importance of Responsibility? This unit helps students understand the importance of responsibility to individuals and to society. Students examine where responsibilities come from and what consequences may result from performing and from not performing responsibilities.

Unit Two: What Might Be Some Benefits and Costs of Fulfilling Responsibilities? This unit helps students understand that when someone fulfills a responsibility, there may be a number of consequences. Some consequences may be advantages, some may be disadvantages. Students learn that it is important to identify benefits and costs when deciding which responsibilities are more important to fulfill.

Unit Three: How Should Conflicts Between Competing Responsibilities Be Resolved? This unit helps students understand that we are often faced with competing responsibilities, values, and interests. Students learn a procedure useful in making reasonable decisions about which responsibilities to fulfill and which values and interests to pursue.

Unit Four: Who Should Be Considered Responsible? This unit helps students learn a procedure useful in evaluating and taking positions on when persons should be considered responsible—when they deserve credit or blame—for an event or situation.

Justice

Unit One: What Is Justice? This unit helps students understand that issues of justice can be divided into three categories: distributive justice, corrective justice, and procedural justice. Students learn to identify issues of justice in terms of these three categories and explain why making these distinctions is important.

Unit Two: What Is Distributive Justice? This unit helps students understand distributive justice, or how fairly benefits or burdens are distributed among persons or groups in society. Students learn that benefits may include pay for work or the right to speak or vote. Burdens may include obligations such as doing homework or paying taxes. Students learn a procedure useful in dealing with such issues.

Unit Three: What Is Corrective Justice? This unit helps students understand corrective justice, or issues of fair or proper responses to wrong and injuries. Students learn a procedure useful in dealing with such issues.

Unit Four: What Is Procedural Justice? This unit helps students understand procedural justice, or the fairness of procedures used to gather information and make decisions. Students learn a procedure useful in dealing with such issues.

While conceptual in nature, *Foundations of Democracy* is based on the day-to-day experiences of students. The uniqueness of the curriculum is that it helps students see the relationship of their experiences to the larger arena of social and political life.

The curriculum is designed to be integrated into American history, government, and other social studies and general humanities courses, including language arts.

Teacher's Guide Format

Unit format. The teacher's guide, like the student book, is organized into units. Each begins with a **Unit Overview**, parallel to the **Purpose of Unit** section of the student text. These provide a brief introduction to the forthcoming group of lessons.

Lesson format. The teacher's guide is designed to complement and extend the student text. Each lesson begins with a **Lesson Overview** to describe the overall purpose of the lesson. Next is a list of **Lesson Objectives**, written in behavioral terms. These parallel the list of behaviors found in the **Purpose of Lesson** in the student text. Students can be expected to be able to perform these tasks upon completing each lesson. The material is conceptually cumulative, however, so mastery is not expected or required at each step along the way.

The lesson objectives are followed by a section titled **Preparation/Materials Required**. This section identifies the applicable pages in the student text and suggests additional preparation or materials needed to teach the lesson. The next section is **Teaching Procedures**. These are suggested instructional strategies which you can adapt to your particular learning environment. They include ideas for introducing the lesson, additional information about lesson topics, discussion questions, and answers to specific student exercises. This section also offers activities and strategies for concluding the lesson.

A section titled **Using the Lesson** completes each section of the guide. This section includes individual, small, and whole group activities designed to reinforce or extend what students have learned in the lesson. The suggestions in this section offer a variety of techniques and develop a number of skills helpful in studying conceptually oriented material. These activities also can easily be adapted as part of the lesson presentation. Where appropriate, **Teacher References** providing additional information or specific court decisions related to the lesson have been included.

Teaching Strategies

The following are the instructional methods recommended for use with the *Foundations of Democracy* student text.

INTELLECTUAL TOOLS FOR ANALYZING ISSUES

Sometimes individuals or institutions face issues which are difficult to analyze or to resolve. In the *Foundations of Democracy* curriculum students are exposed to similar problems. The curriculum provides students with a series of analytical frameworks, or **"intellectual tools,"** to help them think critically and develop reasoned and responsible positions on important issues. The term **intellectual tools** refers to a wide variety of ideas and sets of questions useful in examining and making decisions about issues of authority, privacy, responsibility, and justice. These "tools of the mind," like any good tool, can be useful in a number of ways.

The need for and usefulness of various intellectual tools in analyzing issues of authority, privacy, responsibility, and justice may be made more clear by first looking at how intellectual tools are used in other areas of study. Imagine archaeologists walking across a hillside looking for signs of an ancient village. In their minds they carry a body of knowledge and skills, including facts, ideas, hypotheses, and questions, which enable them to notice and understand things that an untrained person might not see or understand.

While a layperson might walk right over the remains of a site, the archaeologists, armed with their special knowledge, immediately recognize the telltale signs of human habitation. They then use their intellectual tools to systematically gather and process information in order to gain a better understanding of the past.

It is the same with persons trained in the use of the intellectual tools of other disciplines. In each, the trained person has an advantage over the untrained person in understanding certain things, accomplishing certain objectives, or in reaching informed decisions and determining subsequent action. This is true whether one is talking about a master carpenter, a television producer, a political scientist, a judge, or an astronaut.

While the general idea of intellectual tools as a thinking process is consistent throughout the curriculum, the sets of questions vary depending on the type of problem to be resolved. For instance, one would not use the same questioning strategies to deal with issues of authority and issues of justice.

The intellectual tools in this curriculum are reinforced through the use of active learning strategies, by which students develop the personal and group interaction skills required for successful social and political participation in a democracy. The programs of the Center for Civic Education are unique in the training they give students in the use of intellectual tools. The intellectual tools, once learned, may be applied again and again to decisions made throughout one's life.

CONDUCTING CLASS DISCUSSIONS

History of the ideas of authority, privacy, responsibility, and justice has included controversy, debate, evaluation, and reevaluation. So, too, does the study of *Foundations of Democracy*. Effective civic education includes presenting and discussing controversial subject matter which is what makes this curriculum exciting for both students and teachers. Through the discussion process, students develop knowledge, decision-making skills, conflict management experience, and a commitment to citizenship participation.

To ensure that the experience with this curriculum is stimulating and rewarding for both you and your students, you may wish to consider the following suggestions for successful classroom discussion of controversial issues and contemporary topics:

- Emphasize the legitimacy of controversy, compromise, and consensus. They are the lifeblood of a democratic society.

- Try to present the central issues of controversy in tangible form. Make allusions to similar problems and dilemmas students face in their own lives.

- Stress historical antecedents so students can see how similar conflicts have been managed in the past. Acknowledge those times when we have not lived up to the ideals and principles upon which our nation was founded. Examining the interpretation and application of these concepts over time will help students appreciate the fluidity of our constitutional system and the role individual citizens play in helping our nation better realize its goals.

- Emphasize the legitimacy of various viewpoints by encouraging students to examine and present conflicting views in an unbiased fashion. It is incumbent on the teacher to raise any opposing views students may have missed.

- Keep students focused on discussing or dealing with ideas or positions, rather than people. Stress that in controversial issues, reasonable people might very well differ. Encourage students to offer dissenting opinions when they do not agree with the majority—even if they are the only one to dissent.

- Help students identify specific points of agreement or disagreement, places where compromise might be possible, and places where it is unlikely to occur. Emphasize that the outcomes or the decisions which they reach on an issue may not be as important as improving their ability to develop a reasoned decision and to express it in a civil manner, respecting the views of others.

- Conclude, or debrief, an activity or discussion by evaluating the arguments presented and exploring the likely consequences of the various alternatives suggested. An effective debriefing also involves both the teacher and the students in evaluating the process used for conducting a discussion, preparing group work, or presenting a class activity.

Before beginning this program, in which class discussion and sharing of opinions are critical components, you may wish to establish a few basic ground rules. For example:

- When expressing an opinion, always be prepared to justify it.

- Politely and respectfully listen to the opinions of others. You may be called on to tell which one (other than your own) you liked best.

- Everyone will get a chance to talk, but only one person will talk at a time.

- Do not argue against people; argue with reasons and ideas.

- You may change your opinion at any time. Be prepared to share your reasons for doing so.

EFFECTIVE QUESTIONING STRATEGIES

Question and response sequences are an important feature of the curriculum. The effective use of questions is critical to the learning process and requires careful planning. While some questions may be useful to establish how much knowledge students have gained, the primary goal of your questioning strategies should be to help students increase their ability to reach effective, responsible decisions. Therefore, you will want to choose questioning strategies that lead students into analysis of situations and into synthesis and evaluation of concepts, thus enabling them to use skills acquired in this program on a lifelong basis.

There are generally six categories of questions you should consider when planning class discussions. Following is a brief description and example of each:

- **Knowledge.** These questions involve recall of specific facts or information.
  Example: What are the three categories of issues of justice?

- **Comprehension.** This involves the ability to understand the meaning of material.
  This may be shown by translating material from one form to another, and by interpreting material.
  Example: Create a drawing illustrating a person fulfilling a responsibility and the source of that responsibility. What is the central idea of this lesson?

- **Application.** This involves the ability to use learned material in new situations.
  Example: What examples can you cite from your own experience where these ideas apply? How might you use this process to resolve a conflict in the future?

- **Analysis.** This involves the ability to break down material into its component parts.
  This includes identifying the parts and establishing the relationship among the parts.
  Example: What are the consequences of privacy in this situation? Which consequences are advantages and which are disadvantages?

- **Synthesis.** This is the ability to put parts together to form a new whole. The emphasis in on creating new patterns of thought.
  Example: What argument can you make that we should increase the authority of the United States Supreme Court?

- **Evaluation.** This is the ability to judge the value of material for a given purpose.
  This may be a process for choosing among competing responsibilities or deciding whether a law meets the criteria of a good rule.
  Example: How useful were the intellectual tools in helping you decide who should be held responsible for this event? What are the likely consequences of the alternative you have suggested?

It is possible to structure questions so that students listen to and respond to each other and not just to their teacher. Encourage students' active participation in the following ways:

- Pose a question and ask students to discuss the answer with a partner.

- Ask students to clarify their responses. This will benefit themselves as well as others.

- Ask students to extend their own or other students' responses by providing additional facts, information, viewpoints, etc.

- Ask students to generate questions of their own on material just presented in class.

- Pause at least seven seconds after asking a question to allow students time to think.

- Ask students to expand on their responses if they provide short or fragmentary answers.

- Call on more than one student per question.

- Encourage students to react to other students' responses.

- Call on nonvolunteers as well as volunteers.

ENCOURAGING SMALL GROUP LEARNING

The critical thinking exercises in the student text are generally designed as cooperative learning activities with a study partner or in small group environments. Each individual's participation is essential for the successful completion of an exercise. Students are encouraged not only to contribute academically, but to develop and use appropriate interpersonal skills.

Important issues arise for the teacher in planning and implementing cooperative group learning. One such issue concerns the size of groups. Consideration of the research can help you determine the optimum number of students per group within your classroom.

David A. Welton and John T. Mallan in their book *Children and Their World: Teaching Elementary Social Studies*, Fourth Edition, Houghton-Mifflin, 1991, have identified some general behavioral characteristics of differently sized groups:

- **Groups of two.** High exchange of information and a tendency to avoid disagreement are two features of pairs. In case of disagreement, however, deadlock occurs because there is no support within the group for either participant.

- **Groups of three.** Triads tend to be characterized by the power of the majority over the minority of one. However, triads are the most stable group structure with some occasional shifting of coalitions.

- **Groups of even numbers.** More disagreement is prevalent in groups with even numbers of members. This is due to the formation of subgroups of equal size resulting in deadlock.

- **Groups of five.** The most satisfying learning group size seems to be five. There is ease of movement within the group. The 2:3 division provides minority members with support. The group is large enough for stimulation, yet small enough for participation and personal recognition.

- **Groups larger than five.** As group size increases, so does the range of ability, expertise, and skill. However, so do the difficulties in keeping all members on task, ensuring everyone the opportunity to speak, and coordinating group actions.

Another issue teachers face in planning and implementing cooperative group learning is whether to allow groups to self-select or to establish the groups by assignment. David W. Johnson, et al. in *Circles of Learning: Cooperation in the Classroom,* published by the Association for Supervision and Curriculum Development, 1984, describes the following characteristics of groups:

- Student-selected groups are frequently homogeneous with high-achieving students selecting other high achievers, males selecting males, and members of different cultural groups selecting those from similar backgrounds.

- There is often less on-task behavior in student-selected than in teacher-selected groups.

- More creative thinking, more frequent giving and receiving of explanations, and greater perspective-taking in discussion seems to occur in heterogeneous groups.

A useful modification of the select-your-own-groups method is to have students list three peers with whom they would like to work. Place the students with one person they chose and other students selected by the teacher. Careful consideration should be given to building a supportive environment for students no one selects.

You also may want to consider randomly assigning students to groups by having them count off. For example, to establish six groups of five students each in a class of thirty, have the students count off from one to six, repeating the sequence at the end of six. Then, place the "ones" together, the "twos" together and so forth. Once groups have been assembled, you may want to have them work together over a period of time rather than forming new groups for each activity in the student text.

Below are some general recommendations you may want to consider in implementing small group work in your classroom:

- Make sure the students have the skills necessary to do the work. If they do not, you will quickly know because they will not long remain on task.

- Give clear instructions for completing work and check for understanding of the process or procedures to be followed during an activity.

- Allow adequate time to complete the assigned task. Think creatively about ways to constructively occupy groups that finish ahead of the others.

- Be explicit in dealing with management issues. If someone must report to the class on the group's work, be sure there is a process for selecting a reporter.

- Think about how your evaluation strategies are affected by the use of small groups. Develop methods to reward group efforts.

- Monitor group work and act as a resource to guide your students' development.

COMMUNITY RESOURCE PEOPLE

Involvement of people from the community who possess appropriate experiences or expertise can greatly enhance and extend student understanding of the concepts presented in *Foundations of Democracy*. Community resource people can contribute in the following ways:

■ make the lessons come alive by sharing real-life experiences and applications of the ideas under consideration

■ help implement activities in the classroom such as role plays, moot courts, and simulated legislative hearings and debates

■ enrich field experiences by serving as a guide and by responding to questions during visits to places such as court rooms and legislative chambers

■ establish an on-going relationship with a class in which the resource person is available regularly by phone to respond to questions or issues that may arise during a particular lesson

The range of individuals who can serve as resource people is as varied as the community itself. Commonly, this includes police officers, lawyers, judges, legislators, state and local government agents, and professors of political science or law. Some lessons may require expertise in other fields such as medicine, environmental science, or business. Specific types of occupations and individuals are suggested, both in the teacher's guide and the student text, who can enliven and enrich your study of the concepts in *Foundations of Democracy*.

Making the involvement of a community resource person as meaningful as possible requires careful planning. Attention should be given to the following considerations:

■ A resource person's involvement should be relevant to the lesson or concept under consideration.

■ The principal mode of involvement should be interaction and participation with students. A resource person should be asked to assist students in preparing a role-play or moot court arguments. The resource person can act as a judge, serve on a panel with students, or respond to questions about specific details of a lesson. Also, a resource person should participate in the concluding discussion of a lesson or activity.

■ A resource person should offer a balanced picture of the topic, including a variety of perspectives. When objectivity is not possible, you might consider inviting a second resource person to ensure a balanced experience. The guest should also avoid professional jargon and speak as simply as possible.

■ Before a visit by a resource person, students should be well prepared to maximize their thoughtful participation when the visitor is present.

■ Most resource persons are not trained teachers and should not be responsible for classroom management. The teacher should be in attendance during the entire visit. Sometimes it might be necessary for the teacher to give direction to the guest by asking appropriate questions or offering clues that can help the resource person communicate effectively with students.

■ For a successful visit, the resource person should receive a copy of the lesson in advance. Usually, a pre-visit meeting or phone call is useful to help clarify what is expected of the guest.

Owing to busy schedules and the limited length of this program, it is advisable to extend invitations as soon as possible. A committee of students should be responsible for hosting the guests on the day of their visit and for the follow-up thank you letter.

INTERACTIVE TEACHING STRATEGIES

An essential feature of *Foundations of Democracy* is the use of instructional methods which actively involve students in developing and presenting positions on issues related to the concepts of authority, privacy, responsibility, and justice. Students will learn to apply their knowledge to contemporary issues as well as to a variety of socio-political questions. In addition, these learning strategies promote certain dispositions and participatory skills that increase students' capacity to act effectively as citizens in a constitutional democracy. For example, students learn to work cooperatively to reach common goals, to evaluate, take, and defend positions on controversial issues, and to deal with conflicting opinions and positions in a constructive manner. These learning strategies also teach students how government works.

The key learning strategies in this curriculum include, among others, legislative hearings, moot courts, and town meetings. The following material describes these instructional methods and others that are used in the upper elementary and secondary curriculum, and offers specific suggestions for implementation in the classroom.

Legislative Hearing

(Other strategies which use this format include mayor's employment panel, school board hearing, city or town council meeting, and administrative hearing.)

Legislative hearings are held by committees of the United States Congress and other legislative bodies to gather information upon which to base recommendations regarding subjects regulated by law or for which laws are being considered. These hearings are a basic function of legislative branches of government.

Role-playing a legislative hearing provides participants with an opportunity to gain increased understanding of the purpose and procedures of such hearings as well as the roles and responsibilities of committee members. Participants also gain experience in identifying and clarifying the ideas, interests, and values associated with the subject being discussed.

How to Proceed

1. **Clarify topics.** Help students understand the topic of the legislative hearing. The topics are clearly identified in the lessons in the student text and in the teacher's

guide. You also will want to ensure that students understand the role of committees in the legislative process.

2. **Contact resource persons.** Invite a local legislator, local groups, or local chapters of national organizations to serve as resource people on the topic of the hearing.

3. **Assign roles.** Explain to participants the purpose of a legislative hearing and assign the appropriate roles:

   a. **Legislators.** Six legislators is a practical number for a committee, but the number may vary according to class needs. Designate one legislator as the chairperson to preside over the hearing.

   b. **Witnesses.** The number and nature of the witnesses depend on the topic being discussed. The specific roles described in the lessons and in the teacher's guide are designed to present differing points of view on the topic.

   c. **Recorder.** This role is optional. This person will keep a record of the proceedings and present a review or summary of any recommendations that may emerge during the discussions.

   d. **Newspaper reporters.** This role is optional, but is useful in helping students gain insights on the function of the press in the democratic process. Select students to represent newspapers with varying perspectives. Ask them to interview legislators and witnesses, to observe the proceedings, and to write brief articles or editorials about the topic. They should share and discuss their work with the class.

4. **Prepare presentations.** Allow time for participants to prepare for the legislative hearing in accordance with their assigned roles. Specific directions in the student text and teacher's guide coordinate the use of the intellectual tools with student preparation for participation in the activity.

   a. Legislators should identify the key issue(s) and prepare questions to ask each witness.

   b. Witnesses should define their position on the issue(s), prepare an opening statement, anticipate questions from the legislators, and formulate possible responses.

   c. Witnesses may wish to discuss similarities in positions with other witnesses.

   d. When appropriate, have a resource person work with the students or allow students to contact outside resources for assistance in preparing their position on an issue.

5. **Arrange the classroom.** Set up the classroom to resemble a legislative chamber. Include a table for the legislators, a desk for the recorder, and a desk or table for the witnesses. Provide a gavel and nameplates with the students' names and their roles. You may want to arrange the use of a hearing or committee room of a local legislative body.

6. **Conduct the hearing.** The following procedures should be used to conduct this activity:

   a. The committee chairperson calls the hearing to order, announces the purpose of the hearing and the order in which the witnesses will be called to testify.

b. The chairperson calls each witness. The witness makes an opening statement, followed by questions from members of the committee. You may want to establish time limits, usually three to four minutes for openings and five to six minutes for questions from the legislators. Appoint a time keeper to enforce time limitations.

c. The chairperson is the first to question the witness, followed by the other members of the committee. However, a committee member may interrupt to ask a question or make a comment any time during the proceedings.

d. After the witnesses have been heard, the legislators review the testimony, discuss the issue(s) and make recommendations on what their next step(s) will be.

7. **Debrief the activity.** Debriefing questions vary according to the topic. Begin by having the legislators announce their decision. Discuss the facts and arguments presented on the topic and evaluate the strengths and weaknesses of the positions taken. Also ask students to evaluate their experience with the hearing process itself. Conclude the debriefing by having students discuss the effectiveness of this activity as a tool for learning, including how well they performed their role in it. If a resource person assisted with the activity, that person should be included in the concluding discussion.

Legislative Debate

Legislative debate is often used productively in the formulation and development of laws. Role-playing a legislative debate provides participants with an opportunity to increase their understanding of the purpose and value of the power of legislatures to make laws and to debate matters of public policy.

How to Proceed

1. **Clarify topics.** Help students understand the topic of the legislative debate. The topics are clearly identified in the lessons in the student text and in the teacher's guide. You will also want to ensure that students understand the process whereby bills are enacted into law.

2. **Contact resource persons.** Contact state and national legislators or their staff assistants to help serve as resource persons.

3. **Assign roles.** Consider the entire class as the legislative body with a student or the teacher assuming the role of the presiding officer. Legislators may then be assigned to groups representing various positions in regard to the issue. Groups are clearly identified in the student text and in the teacher's guide. You may want to assign a recorder responsible for tracking key points of discussion during the debate.

4. **Prepare presentations.** Allow time for participants to prepare for the legislative hearing in accordance with their assigned roles. Specific directions in the lessons in the student text and teacher's guide coordinate the use of the intellectual tools with student preparation for participation in this activity.

   Each group should select a spokesperson and a recorder and then proceed to follow the directions given in the lesson. Students should analyze and evaluate the issue before developing their positions. In some cases they will be asked to offer amendments to the bills already given in the lesson. In others they may write a proposed bill designed to alleviate problems raised by the issue.

As each group completes its amendment or proposed bill, the spokesperson reports to the presiding officer asking that the bill be placed on the agenda. Bills should be placed on the agenda in the order in which they are received. Students may wish to discuss any similarities in their proposed amendments or bills with other groups to predetermine whether they can unite behind a common proposal.

5. **Arrange the classroom.** Set up the classroom to resemble a legislative chamber. Include a table for the presiding officer, a desk for the recorder, and a podium if you want to have presentations made more formally. Provide a gavel and nameplates with the students' names and their roles. You may want to arrange the use of a legislative chamber in your community.

6. **Conduct the legislative debate.** Time limits for the various steps in legislative debates should be decided ahead of time. The presiding officer should be empowered to cut off speakers when the time limit has been reached. Conduct the legislative debate using the following procedures:

   a. The presiding officer calls the legislature to order, indicates that all votes will be decided by a simple majority, announces the issue, and opens the debate.

   b. The first bill on the agenda is introduced by the group's spokesperson. The spokesperson stands, addresses the presiding officer, and describes the bill the group has written. After the presenting the bill, the spokesperson may recognize two other members of the group who may make additional comments on the bill.

   c. The bill is discussed and debated by the legislature. Representatives from other groups may ask questions, offer criticisms, or suggest modifications.

   d. The steps above are repeated for any additional bills that might be introduced during the session.

   e. When the discussion and debate on all proposed bills is completed, legislators may move: (1) that one of the bills be voted on, (2) that the session be recessed to enable the groups to consider the bills that have been presented. If the session is recessed, each group meets to decide upon a course of action. A group may decide to support one of the bills as presented, suggest amendments to one of the bills presented, or develop a compromise bill.

   f. When the session is reconvened, the presiding officer asks for a motion to vote on one of the bills as presented, for a motion to amend one of the bills, or for the introduction of a compromise bill. If amendments or compromise bills are proposed, they are individually debated and voted upon.

   g. This process is repeated until a bill is passed or the time allotted for the session is up and the legislature is adjourned.

7. **Debrief the activity.** Debriefing questions vary according to the topic. Discuss the facts and arguments presented on the topic and evaluate the strengths and weaknesses of the positions taken. Also ask students to evaluate their experience with the legislative process itself. Conclude the debriefing by having students discuss the effectiveness of this activity as a tool for learning, including how well they performed their role in it. If a resource person assisted with the activity, that person should be included in the concluding discussion.

Pro Se Court

A *pro se* (or do it yourself) court allows students to role-play a court case with a minimum of participants and simple rules of evidence. The court is organized as a triad consisting of a judge, who will hear the two sides and make the final decision; a plaintiff, who is the person bringing the action before the judge; and the defendant, who is accused of wrongdoing or causing injury.

Pro se courts provide students with a simplified look at judicial decision making. *Pro se* courts provide an opportunity for all students in a class to be actively involved in the activity.

How to Proceed

1. **Clarify topic.** Help students understand the facts and issues in the case. The cases are clearly identified in the lessons in the student text and in the teacher's guide.

2. **Contact resource person.** Invite an attorney or judge to act as a resource person.

3. **Assign roles.** Divide the class into three equal groups—judges, plaintiffs, and defendants.

4. **Prepare presentations.** Have the students meet in their respective groups to help each other prepare their presentations. Each student will be actively involved in the role play, so preparation at this stage is vital to effective participation in the activity. Specific directions in the lessons in the student text and teacher's guide coordinate the use of the intellectual tools with student preparation for participation in this activity.

   Instruct the judges to review the case and the issues raised. Ask them to prepare questions that they would like to ask of the plaintiffs and defendants during the presentation phase of the activity. The questions should be designed to clarify positions on the issues which the judges will be called upon to decide. Do take some time to review with the judge's group some simple rules of procedure, like the following:

   a. The plaintiff should present first, without interruptions from the defense. The defense presents their case second.

   b. Allow brief rebuttals from each side in the case.

   c. The judge may interrupt the presentations at any time to pose questions designed to clarify the arguments being made.

   Instruct the plaintiff and defendant groups to prepare an opening statement and arguments supporting their positions on the issues raised in the case.

5. **Arrange the classroom.** You will have multiple courts in session simultaneously; therefore, arrange the desks in the classroom into groups of three, one for each of the roles in the activity.

6. **Conduct the court hearing.** Before beginning the activity, match one student from the judge's group with one student from the plaintiff and one from the defendant groups. You may want to have the judges first take a desk in each of the groupings arranged around the room. Then ask one plaintiff and one defendant to join the group. Matching role-players may be more easily accomplished by providing role "tags" so students can quickly identify who is a judge, plaintiff, and defendant.

   Conduct the activity using the following procedures:

   a. Instruct the judges that when each has a plaintiff and a defendant, he or she may begin the court session.

b. The judge should first hear opening statements by the participants—first the plaintiff and then the defendant. An appropriate time limit should be imposed on these statements.

c. The plaintiff makes arguments and is questioned by the judge.

d. The defendant presents his or her defense and is questioned by the judge.

e. The judge asks each side for brief rebuttal statements.

f. The judge makes his or her decision and explains the reasoning which supports it.

7. **Debrief the activity.** Debriefing questions vary according to the topic. Begin by asking individual judges to share with the class their decision and the reasoning supporting it. Discuss the facts and arguments presented in the case and evaluate the strengths and weaknesses of the positions taken. Also ask students to evaluate the court process itself. Conclude the debriefing by having students discuss the effectiveness of this activity as a tool for learning, including how well they performed their role in it. If a resource person assisted with the activity, that person should be included in the concluding discussion.

Moot Court

A moot court is patterned on an appeals court or Supreme Court hearing. The court, composed of a panel of judges or justices, is asked to rule on a lower court's decision. No witnesses are called, nor are the basic facts in a case disputed. Arguments are prepared and presented on the application of a law, the constitutionality of a law, or the fairness of previous court procedures. In many ways the moot court is like a debate, for each side presents arguments for the consideration of the justices.

Since moot courts are not concerned with the credibility of witness testimony, they are an effective strategy for focusing student attention on the underlying principles and concepts of authority, privacy, responsibility, and justice.

How to Proceed

1. **Clarify topic.** Help students understand the facts and the legal or constitutional issues in the case. The cases are clearly identified in the lessons in the student text and in the teacher's guide. You may also want to ensure that students understand the purpose and procedures observed in appellate court proceedings.

2. **Contact resource persons.** Invite an attorney or judge to act as a resource person.

3. **Assign roles.** Assign students to play the roles of justices of the court (in intermediate appellate courts members of the panel are called judges. In the federal or state supreme courts they are called justices). You may establish a court of five, seven, or nine justices. Divide the remaining students into two teams representing the litigants in the case. One team will represent the person or group bringing the challenge before the court, or the plaintiff. The other team will represent the person or group defending against the challenge, or the defendant. Sometimes terms like petitioner or respondent, or appellant and appellee, are used to identify the litigants in an appellate case. For pedagogical purposes, it is best to keep it simple by using the terms plaintiff and defendant.

4. **Prepare presentations.** Each team should meet to prepare arguments for its side of the case. The team should select one or two students to present the arguments. Specific directions in the lessons in the student text and teacher's guide coordinate the use of the intellectual tools with student preparation for participation in this activity.

   The justices should meet to discuss the issues involved and any questions they feel need to be addressed in order for them to reach a decision. The justices should select one student to serve as chief justice. The chief justice will preside over the hearing. He or she will call on each side to present its case or (more realistically) justices (judges) should ask questions without needing to be recognized (i.e., judges should feel free to interrupt lawyers' presentations whenever they want).

   Participants should take it as given that the factual details presented in the summary of the case were established by a trial and are not subject to further dispute.

   Arguments should not concentrate on legal technicalities. Any argument that is persuasive from a philosophical, theoretical, conceptual, or practical standpoint can be made. Teams should rely on principles found or implied in the United States Constitution.

5. **Arrange the classroom.** Set up the classroom to resemble an appellate court. The justices should be seated at a table at the front of the room. The attorneys for each side should sit on opposite sides of the room facing the justices. Other team members should sit behind their respective attorneys. You may want to take the class to an appellate courtroom or to a mock trial room at a law school.

6. **Conduct the moot court.** The chief justice should preside over the proceedings and begin by calling the court to order. The chief justice should observe the following procedures:

   a. Each side should be allotted five to ten minutes for the initial presentation and five minutes for rebuttal. The chief justice should call for presentations in the following order:

      | Plaintiff | Initial presentation |
      | Defendant | Initial presentation |
      | Plaintiff | Rebuttal presentation |
      | Defendant | Rebuttal presentation |

   b. During and/or after each presentation, the justices can and should actively question the attorneys in an effort to clarify the arguments. Attorneys may request time to consult with other members of their team before answering questions. For clarity and continuity, it is suggested that during the initial presentations lawyers be given three minutes to present their cases before being interrupted with questions.

   c. After arguments have been presented, the justices should organize themselves in a circle. They should consider the arguments and make a decision by a majority vote. Each justice should give reasons for his or her position. The rest of the class may sit outside of the circle and listen, but they may not talk or interrupt the deliberations.

7. **Debrief the activity.** Debriefing questions vary according to the case. Begin by asking the justices to share with the class their decision and the reasoning supporting it. Justices should present dissenting opinions. Discuss the arguments presented in the case and evaluate the strengths and weaknesses of the positions taken. Also ask students to evaluate their experience with the appellate process itself. Conclude the debriefing by having students discuss the effectiveness of this activity as a tool for learning, including how well they performed their role in it. If a resource person assisted with the activity, that person should be included in the concluding discussion.

In an actual case, you should share the Court's decision with the class during the debriefing. In order to dispel the notion that there in one "right" answer, also share relevant parts of the dissenting opinion. Help students understand the reasoning which supports both the majority and dissenting opinions.

Mediation

In a mediation session an impartial person or agency helps settle controversies or disputes between opposing interests, such as labor and management or litigants in a law suit. Mediators meet with leaders from both sides and attempt to facilitate communications, promote understanding and clarification of issues, and effect an agreement or resolution satisfactory to both parties. The mediator(s) have no authority to force agreements.

This type of role-play promotes student understanding of alternative methods of dispute resolution and an understanding that not all disagreements need to be settled in a court of law.

How to Proceed

1. **Clarify topic.** Help students understand the facts in the dispute. The cases are clearly identified in the lessons in the student text and in the teacher's guide. You may also want to ensure that students understand the purpose of mediation, how mediation differs from the adversarial process, and the procedures observed in mediation sessions.

2. **Contact resource persons.** Invite a mediator or an attorney to act as a resource person.

3. **Assign Roles.** Divide the class into three equal groups representing mediators and the disputing parties.

4. **Prepare presentations.** Have the students meet in their respective groups to help each other prepare for their mediation sessions. Each student will be actively involved in the role-play, so preparation at this stage is vital to effective participation in the activity. Specific directions in the lessons in the student text and teacher's guide coordinate the use of the intellectual tools with student preparation for participation in this activity.

Instruct the mediators to review the facts in the dispute and then to prepare for acting out their roles. Do take time to review with the mediators the procedures for mediating a dispute. Mediators should follow the following instructions:

a. Introduce the parties to the dispute and explain the mediation process. Let them know that no one will force them to settle the dispute. Your role is to guide the session and to ensure that everyone can speak openly.

b. Help the parties tell about the dispute. Ask open ended questions like, "What happened next?" Listen carefully. No one should interrupt while another person is speaking.

c. Do not try to determine who is at fault in the dispute. Look for concerns and interests the parties have in common. Help them see the good in their relationship and remind them that they may want to maintain the relationship in the future.

d. Help the parties identify ways to settle their dispute. Help them evaluate alternative solutions to the problem.

e. Help the parties write an agreement that clearly spells out the responsibilities of the parties in the agreed upon solution.

Instruct the disputing parties to prepare what they might want to say during the mediation session. Ask them to think about issues where they might be willing to compromise.

5. **Arrange the classroom.** You will have multiple mediation groups working simultaneously; therefore, arrange the desks in the classroom into groups of three, one for each of the roles in the activity.

6. **Conduct the mediation.** Before beginning the activity, match one student from the mediator's group with one student from each of the disputing party's groups. You may want to have the mediators first take a desk in each of the groupings arranged around the room. Then ask one student from each of the disputing parties to join the group. Matching role-players may be more easily accomplished by providing role "tags" so students can quickly identify who is a mediator and who are role-playing disputants. You may want to prepare some additional activity for those groups that finish early.

Conduct the activity using the following procedures:

a. **Introduction.** The mediator sets the parties at ease and explains the ground rules. The mediator explains that his/her role is not to take sides, but to help both parties reach a mutual agreement.

b. **Telling the story.** Each party tells what happened. The person making the complaint tells his or her side of the story first. No interruptions are allowed.

c. **Identifying facts and issues.** The mediator attempts to identify agreed upon facts and issues. This is done by listening to each side, summarizing each party's views, and asking if these are the facts and issues as each party understands them.

d. **Identifying alternative solutions.** Everyone thinks of possible solutions to the problem. The mediator makes a list and asks each party to explain his or her feelings about each possible solution. Based on the expressed feelings of the parties, the mediator revises possible solutions and attempts to identify a solution that both parties can agree to.

e. **Reaching agreement.** The mediator helps the parties to reach an agreement that both can live with. The agreement should be written down. The parties should also discuss what will happen if either of them breaks the agreement.

7. **Debrief the activity.** Debriefing questions vary according to the issues in the dispute. Begin by asking individual mediators to describe the agreements reached in their group. If a group reached an impasse, ask the mediator to explain what seemed to be the obstacles to an agreement. Ask students to evaluate the strength of the positions taken and of the procedures used to develop and support a position. Also ask students to evaluate their experience with the mediation process itself. Conclude the debriefing by having students discuss the effectiveness of this activity as a tool for learning, including how well they performed their role in it. If a resource person assisted with the activity, that person should be included in the concluding discussion.

Town Meeting

A town meeting provides members of a community with an opportunity to participate in the decision-making process. A community forum usually considers matters of public policy. A town meeting can serve as a local governing and decision-making body by performing functions similar to those of a representative town or city council. It can also be advisory in nature, providing elected representatives with the views of citizens.

How to Proceed

1. **Clarify topic.** Help students understand the topic of the town meeting. The topics are clearly identified in the lessons in the student text and in the teacher's guide. You also will want to ensure that students understand the nature and purpose of a town meeting.

2. **Contact resource person.** Invite a member of the city council or a local interest group to serve as a resource person on the topic of the meeting.

3. **Assign roles.** Organize the town meeting by assigning individuals the following roles:
   a. chairperson
   b. elected officials who represent the entire community in the town or city council
   c. representative groups in favor of the proposition
   d. representative groups in opposition to the proposition
   e. community members at large
   f. recorder

4. **Prepare presentations.** Allow time for students to prepare for the town meeting in accordance with their assigned roles. Specific directions in the student text and teacher's guide coordinate the use of the intellectual tools with student preparation for participation in this activity.

5. **Arrange the classroom.** Include a table for the chairperson and for the elected officials, a desk for the recorder, and a podium from which members of interest groups and the community can speak. Provide a gavel and nameplates with the students' names and their roles. You may want to arrange the use of a hearing or committee room of a local legislative body.

6. **Conduct the town meeting.** The following procedures should be used to conduct this activity:

   a. The chairperson calls the meeting to order, announces the purpose of the meeting, and introduces the elected officials in attendance. Elected officials may make a brief opening statement about the importance of the issue being considered (not his or her personal views on the topic). The chairperson also establishes any rules that are to be followed during the meeting, such as time limits for presentations.

   b. The chairperson has the authority to cut off debate when time limits have been reached. A person may not speak unless recognized by the chair, and no one may interrupt while another person is speaking. If a speaker wanders from the point, abuses other people, or in any way defeats the purpose of the meeting, the chairperson may declare him or her out of order.

   c. The chairperson calls upon a representative of the group favoring the proposition to describe that group's position. After the representative has finished speaking, he or she may ask people brought as witnesses to stand and speak. The chairperson announces that any person in favor of the proposition may stand and speak. They will be recognized in the order in which they stand. Alternatively, you may want to have students sign in and ask the chairperson to recognize speakers by the order in which they signed in.

   d. The chairperson calls upon a representative of the group opposed to the proposition to speak. After the representative has finished speaking, he or she may ask people brought as witnesses to stand and speak. The chairperson announces that those people opposed to the proposition will be recognized in the order in which they stand.

   e. After all people on both sides of the proposition have had an opportunity to speak, the chairperson opens the question for additional discussion or debate. During this time any person may stand, be recognized, and present his or her point of view or argue against the point of view of someone else.

   f. At the end of the discussion or debate the chairperson calls for class vote on the proposition. The vote is decided by a majority.

7. **Debrief the activity.** Debriefing questions vary according to the topic. Begin by discussing the results of the vote taken on the proposition. Discuss the facts and argument presented on the topic. Ask students to evaluate the strength of the positions taken and of the procedures used to develop and support a position. Also ask students to evaluate their experience with the town meeting itself. Conclude the debriefing by having students discuss the effectiveness of this activity as a tool for learning, including how well they performed their role in it. If a resource person assisted with the activity, that person should be included in the concluding discussion.

Debates

Debate begins with the assumption that the debater has already found a solution or approach to a specific issue. The intent of the debater is to persuade others that his or her solution or approach is the proper one.

Debate can be an effective device for encouraging students to clearly and logically formulate arguments based upon evidence. Debate teaches a means to adequately support a position on an issue. It also develops a sense of efficacy and confidence in a person's ability to sway public opinion or to change public policy.

How to Proceed

1. **Clarify topic.** Help students understand the topic of the debate. The topics are clearly identified in the lessons in the student text and in the teacher's guide. Formulate the topic into a resolution (resolutions always ask for a change from the status quo, e.g., Resolved: that capital punishment should be found unconstitutional by the United States Supreme Court).

2. **Contact resource person.** Invite someone from the community or a local interest group to serve as a resource person on the topic of the debate.

3. **Assign roles.** Select students to take part in the debate. Divide them into two teams, one in support of the resolution, the other opposing it. Make certain that those participating in the debate are familiar with the procedures to be followed during the debate. Select a moderator and a time keeper.

4. **Prepare presentations.** Allow sufficient time for students to prepare their "constructive arguments" (argument based upon three to five major points logically developed and substantiated by factual evidence in support of a particular position). Help students see the dimensions of the problem and develop clear, logical arguments supported by evidence on the position they defend in the debate. Also, ask them to anticipate the views of the other side in preparation for their "rebuttal arguments."

   Help students gain an understanding of some of the implicit values in debate such as learning to make convincing arguments from another frame of reference, as might be the case if one is debating a position that does not correspond with one's own beliefs. This furthers development of students' abilities to understand and respect the right of individuals to hold opinions and beliefs that are different from their own.

5. **Arrange the classroom.** The moderator and debaters are seated at the front of the audience, usually with the team in opposition to the resolution to the left of the moderator.

6. **Conduct the debate.** The form of debate described here is widely used, but is rather formalized. You may wish to make the procedures less formal or use some other form of debate.

   a. The moderator briefly introduces the subject and the resolution to be debated and establishes the time limits to be observed by the speakers.

   b. The moderator introduces the first speaker from the affirmative team and asks the speaker to present his or her constructive argument. The order in which constructive arguments will be given by each member of the team should be determined in advance of the debate. The time keeper will inform the speaker when the time limit has been reached.

   c. The moderator introduces the first speaker from the team in opposition to the resolution and asks the speaker to present his or her constructive argument.

   d. The moderator next introduces the second speaker from the affirmative team. This procedure is alternated until each debater on both affirmative and opposition teams have given a constructive argument.

e. Rebuttal arguments follow the constructive arguments. At this time each debater is given the opportunity to weaken the position of the opponents by attacking their position and by answering attacks that have been made upon his or her position. No new issues may be introduced during rebuttal arguments. Rebuttal arguments always begin with the team in opposition to the resolution. Again, follow the same alternating procedures used during constructive arguments.

f. At the conclusion of the debate, the moderator makes a few concluding remarks and the debate is ended.

7. **Debrief the activity.** You may wish to evaluate the success of the debating teams by informally polling the class to determine how many people agree with the team in support of the resolution and how many agree with the team in opposition to the resolution. You may then ask class members to explain whether their own positions were strengthened or changed as a result of hearing the debate and why. Also ask students to evaluate their experience with the debate process itself. Conclude the debriefing by having students discuss the effectiveness of this activity as a tool for learning, including how well they performed their role in it. If a resource person assisted with the activity, that person should be included in the concluding discussion.

Continuum

The continuum is an exercise in which participants are presented with a range of possible attitudes or approaches on a controversial issue. Participants are asked to determine which element of the continuum (e.g., strongly agree or strongly disagree) most approximates their own attitude. Issues that are clearly controversial and characterized by polar position are suitable for using this method. The issues should have legitimate opposing view points, such as whether equal rights can best be achieved by an amendment or whether gun control is an effective way to stop crime. Issues that are above debate such as the morality of a holocaust or sexual abuse of children are obviously not legitimate topics for a continuum.

The continuum is a useful tool for introducing controversial issues. It can help students see the ranges of values or opinions which exist on a given topic and understand the reasoning which supports those positions. The continuum provides an orderly method for discussing controversy, especially at the early stages of a lesson when students may be expressing "gut-level" reactions rather than informed opinions.

How to Proceed

1. Identify an issue to be discussed. The issue should be one in which one can identify polar positions, such as the death penalty.

2. Before initiating the activity it is important to cultivate a classroom atmosphere of trust where opinions can be expressed freely. Being receptive and non-judgmental is critical to open discussion.

3. The teacher should initiate the activity by describing the issue(s) in enough detail so that the polar positions are clearly understood. These should be written on the board.

4. Students should be asked to write their position on the issue (e.g., strongly agree, agree, can't decide, disagree, strongly disagree) and to list the two most compelling reasons why they believe as they do.

5. While the students are writing their statements, the teacher can draw a continuum line across the chalkboard. When the students are finished writing, the teacher can print along the continuum brief versions of some possible polar position on the issue. Ask a limited number of students to stand at the position on the continuum where they believe their position on the issue falls.

6. At this point, students should be asked to explain or clarify, but not to defend their positions. They should be encouraged to move their position along the continuum as they listen to others clarify their positions.

7. Students now can be asked to state their reasons for positioning themselves as they have. The teacher may wish to post on the board the different reasons expressed by the students. At this point, students can respond to questions concerning their reasoning, but argumentation should be discouraged.

8. In order to assure that students listen to and consider opposing points of view, all students should be asked to present the arguments that, although contrary to their positions, give them pause, make them think twice, or are the most persuasive.

9. Finally, students should be asked to consider the consequences of alternative policy choices. This involves identifying the existing law or policy on the issue being considered, if one exists. The class can then discuss what impact the polar positions presented on the continuum would have on society as a whole and on individuals.

Keeping Journals

Journal writing provides a systematic way for students to maintain a personal record of summary statements, reflections, or questions about what is being learned in a particular instance. Journal writing encourages students to reflect on the "what," "why," and "how" of their own learning. Taking time to reflect is a good study habit to develop. Journals have the additional benefit of improving writing skills.

Because the content introduced in *Foundations of Democracy* contains many new concepts and experiences, opportunities for students to reflect on what they are learning are especially important. Some opportunities for journal writing are identified in the teacher's guide, but many more exist in this curriculum. You may want to allow a few minutes at the conclusion of a lesson or at the close of an activity for students to complete a journal entry. Encourage students to discuss some aspect of the content studied, to record a personal reaction to the lesson or the outcome of an activity, or to record questions the lesson or activity raised about an issue. Sometimes you may want to assign journal notations as homework.

Whether or not to grade journals is a personal choice. However, you should periodically collect journals to offer students some feedback on the content. Writing comments and personal observations in the journals can be an effective tool in establishing a personal dialogue with students. Do encourage students to share their journals with other students and with their parents if they wish. By so doing, students demonstrate to themselves and others what they have learned.

Evaluating Student Achievement

The methods used to evaluate student achievement of the sophisticated concepts, knowledge, and skills offered in the *Foundations of Democracy* curriculum need to be both comprehensive and varied. The methods selected for measuring progress may range from the more traditional paper and pencil tests to performance-based assessments.

Traditional paper and pencil tests are valuable for checking knowledge and understanding of specific concepts, ideas, or procedures. Teachers who engage students in activities requiring complex knowledge and skills, however, need to measure achievement in a similar context. For example, students who participate in a simulated legislative hearing should be asked to demonstrate their knowledge and skills in a similar and equal context. This is what makes performance assessment so well suited for measuring achievement during interactive learning strategies.

Performance assessment differs from traditional tests in that students are not asked to recognize and select correct answers to questions focused on discreet, isolated facts. During performance assessment, students demonstrate their knowledge and skills by addressing complex questions within a meaningful context (e.g., a legislative hearing) for which there is usually not just one correct answer. Students, therefore, construct or create appropriate answers, or a product, as a means of demonstrating what they know and what they can do.

Performance assessment is particularly well suited to the content, skills, and learning experiences emphasized in *Foundations of Democracy*. Classroom activities such as group discussions, moot courts, debates, and other creative projects provide prime opportunities for integrating performance assessment as part of the learning. The units of study within the text are organized so that the final lesson(s) in the unit provides a meaningful context in which students can demonstrate the knowledge and skills gained. Additionally, the final lesson in each concept is a culminating activity requiring application of the total learning experience within that concept. Other opportunities for integrating performance assessment may be found in each lesson in the section titled "Using the Lesson."

Below are some general recommendations you may want to consider in designing your evaluation of student achievement in this program:

- Assess desired behavior in the context in which the behavior is used. To assess students' ability to do **X**, have them do **X**.

- Assess how well students can apply what they learned in one situation by asking them to apply similar knowledge and skills in other, similar situations. Structure situations in which students can construct or create appropriate answers, rather than select from a menu of choices.

- Assess the process and the quality of a performance or product, not the ability to identify correct answers. Stress the thinking and reasoning that supports a quality performance or product.

- Assess how well students see the connections among a variety of related ideas and skills. For example, in preparing for a debate students should combine reading, research, writing, speaking, and critical thinking skills. Students also should see how knowledge and skills from other disciplines can help them deal with challenging topics.

- Provide the criteria for successful performance in advance and make sure that they are clearly understood. When possible provide models of exemplary performance.

- Provide criteria for effective and successful group work. Teamwork and group interaction are important skills that are given legitimacy when students know they are being assessed.

- Structure opportunities for students to assess their own progress, to judge for themselves when they have or have not done well. This will help them internalize high standards and learn to judge for themselves when they measure up. Because most learning strategies in this text are used more than once, students will have successive opportunities to reflect on their progress.

- Offer plenty of opportunities for students to receive feedback from the teacher, their peers, and community resource people who participate in activities with the class.

Reflecting on the Learning Experience

At the conclusion of each lesson and each unit of study in *Foundations of Democracy* the teacher's guide recommends that students evaluate the extent to which they achieved the objectives of that particular lesson or unit. Additionally, it can be valuable to both you and your students to reflect upon and evaluate the total experience upon completing each of the concepts of authority, privacy, responsibility, and justice, or upon completing the entire curriculum. This includes thinking about the content as well as the instructional methods used to learn about that concept.

At the conclusion of each concept (or the entire curriculum), distribute a copy of the following "Reflecting on Your Experience" handout to each student. Ask students to respond to the questions. Remind them that they should not only reflect on and evaluate their own learning experiences, but also those of the entire class. Conduct a class discussion in which students have an opportunity to share their reflections on the learning experiences offered in *Foundations of Democracy*.

Reflecting on Your Experience

It is always a good idea to think about, or reflect upon, experiences you have had or projects you have completed. That is one way to learn, to avoid mistakes in the future, and to improve your performance.

Now that your class has completed this study, you have an opportunity to reflect upon or evaluate what and how you and your classmates learned. You also have an opportunity to think about what you might do differently if you were to study other topics similar to this.

Use the following questions to help you reflect upon and evaluate your experience:

1. What did **I** personally learn about issues we studied from working with my classmates?_____
   _____
   _____

2. What did **we** as a class learn about the issues from the reading, the class discussions,
   and critical thinking exercises?_____
   _____
   _____

3. What skills did **I** learn or improve upon as a result of this experience?_____
   _____
   _____

4. What skills did the **class** learn or improve upon as a result of this experience?_____
   _____
   _____

5. What are the **disadvantages** of working with study partners and in small groups?_____
   _____
   _____

6. What are the **advantages** of working with study partners and in small groups? _____
   _____
   _____

7. What did **I** do well?_____
   _____
   _____

8. What would **I** want to do differently the next time I study a topic similar to this? _____
   _____
   _____

9. What did **we**, as a class, do well? _____
   _____
   _____

10. What would **we** want to do differently the next time we study a topic similar to this? _____
   _____
   _____

The Authority Curriculum

Introduce the Authority curriculum. Begin by reminding students that authority touches the lives of everyone in society—parents, teachers, students, judges, legislators, presidents, and police officers. Some people might view authority as unnecessary, even antithetical to freedom and human dignity; however, most people see authority as essential to civilization and valuable to social existence. Americans have often displayed a distrust of authority, but have looked to authority for the resolution of conflict and the maintenance of order. Our Constitution clearly reflects this fundamental ambivalence. While the Constitution provides for authority, it also limits its practice.

Have the class read the "Introduction" on p. 2 of the student text. Discuss the meaning of the quotation from the Declaration of Independence with the class. Help them identify "consent of the governed" as the source of authority for our government. Ask students to identify some ways citizens influence our government's use of the authority we have given it. Explain to the class that this study will help them gain a better understanding of the purposes and uses of authority and increase their ability to deal effectively with issues of authority that arise in their daily lives as citizens in a free society.

Unit One: What Is Authority?

Introduce **Unit One: What Is Authority?** Explain that in this unit the class will discuss issues that can help them better understand the relevance of authority to their daily lives and to common controversies in their community, state, nation, and world.

Direct attention to the illustration on p. 3 of the student text. Ask students to respond to the question in the caption, "What examples of authority do these pictures illustrate?" Ask students to identify examples of authority from their experiences. Record their responses on the board. Explain that in studying this unit they will learn to define authority and to explain where authority can be found. Students will learn to identify the sources of authority and to recognize that sources of authority often exist in hierarchies. For example, one might trace the source of the authority of a teacher to the school administration, then to the school board, a state law, the state constitution, and ultimately, to the consent of the governed.

Have the class read "Purpose of Unit" on p. 3 of the text. Ask students to list four things they expect to learn from their study of Unit One. If students are keeping a journal during their study of this curriculum, they can record what they expect to learn from this unit in their journals. This activity should be repeated during the introductions to Units Two, Three, and Four.

Lesson 1: What Is the Difference Between Authority and Power Without Authority?

Teaching Procedures

A. Introducing the Lesson

While you post the "Terms to Know" on the board, have the class read "Purpose of Lesson" on p. 4 of the text. Direct class discussion to the terms **power** and **authority**. Ask one-half of the students to think about the meaning of the word "power" and the other half to think about the meaning of the word "authority." Then ask students to share their thoughts with the class. On the board, post the definitions students suggest. Leave the definitions on the board for future reference.

B. Critical Thinking Exercise
Identifying the Difference Between Power and Authority

Have the class read the critical thinking exercise, "Identifying the Difference Between Power and Authority," on p. 4 of the text. The reading selection, "A Dangerous Ride," describes a situation that occurred on the subway late one evening when two teenagers dressed in gang colors boarded the train. Conduct a class discussion in which students respond to the questions in the "What do you think?" section on p. 4 of the text.

C. Reading and Discussion
What are power and authority?

Have the class read "What are power and authority?" on p. 4 of the text. Ask students to compare the definitions of power and authority that they created earlier in the lesson with those they just read in the text. Review each of the examples of power and authority presented on pp. 4-5 of the text with the class. Ask students to suggest additional examples of power and authority from their experience. Ask students to explain whether the examples of authority they suggest might be justified on the basis of either **customs, laws,** or **principles of morality**.

D. Critical Thinking Exercise
Identifying the Use of Authority and the Use of Power Without Authority

Have students work with a study partner to examine each of the nine hypothetical situations described on pp. 5-6 of the text. Have them classify each situation as an example of either authority or power without authority. Ask students to record their responses on paper and to be prepared to share them with the class. Allow adequate time for students to complete their work and then ask them to share their responses with the class.

Students most likely will identify items number 1, 2, 3, 4, 6, 7, and 9 as examples of authority. However, item number 7 may be an example of abuse of authority, i.e., exercise of power beyond limits of authority. Since authority of the city council is limited by the Constitution, refusal to permit a protest rally may violate the First Amendment. Items number 5 and 8 are examples of power without authority. Item number 8 raises the issue of the limits of civil disobedience, and provides the opportunity to discuss acceptable means of communicating dissent and each individual's right of authority to peaceably petition for redress of grievances. Help students understand that individuals who exercise power over others and who have the right to do so are exercising authority. Students also should understand that individuals who exercise power over others without the right to do so according to custom, law, or principles of morality are exercising power without authority.

E. Concluding the Lesson

Direct attention to the illustrations on pp. 4-5 of the text. Ask students to respond to the questions in the captions:

- Who in this picture has the right to use power?
- Where do teachers get their authority?
- What authority do school principals have?

Next, direct students to question number 3 in "Examining the Situations" on page 6:

- Why do students think it is important to know the difference between power and authority?

- How might this be beneficial in their own lives?
- How might it be helpful to a citizen in a free society?

Have students re-read "Purpose of Lesson" on p. 4 of the text. Ask them to describe the extent to which they achieved the objectives of the lesson.

Using the Lesson

The activities suggested in "Using the Lesson" on p. 6 of the text reinforce or extend what students have learned about defining authority and identifying situations in which someone is exercising authority or power without authority.

Suggestion number 1 directs students to keep a journal during their study of authority. During various lessons in this curriculum, students will be instructed to record their ideas, observations, or personal feelings in their journals. Suggestion number 2 introduces students to a practice they will follow in several lessons: expanding their understanding of a concept by analyzing newspaper or television reports of current events. You may have students complete these exercises by working individually or in small groups. Ask students to share their work with the class.

Lesson 2: Why Do We Need Authority?

Lesson Overview

This lesson illustrates problems that are likely to arise in the absence of effective authority. Students examine the problems created by a lack of effective authority described in Mark Twain's *Roughing It*. They learn that we use authority to protect our rights, to provide order and security, to manage conflict, and to distribute the benefits and burdens of society. In a final exercise, students examine how authority was used to include female students in the athletic program at an imaginary school.

Lesson Objectives

At the conclusion of this lesson, students should be able to do the following:

- identify problems likely to arise from a lack of effective authority

- explain how authority might be used to solve problems and promote change

- evaluate the use of authority in solving particular problems

Preparation/Teaching Materials

Student text pp. 7-10

Teaching Procedures

A. Introducing the Lesson

Ask the class to imagine participating in a football game, or any other game, without any rules of play. Ask students to identify problems that might arise. Record their responses on the board. Ask students if they would want to participate in such a game. Explain that during this lesson the class will examine some problems likely to arise in situations where there is an absence of rules or other effective authority.

While you post the "Terms to Know" on the board, have students read "Purpose of Lesson" on p. 7 of the student text.

B. Reading and Discussion
What might happen if there were no authority?

Have the class read "What might happen if there were no authority?" on p. 7 of the text. Ask the students to respond to the questions in the "What do you think?" section.

C. Critical Thinking Exercise
Identifying Uses of Authority

Have students work with a study partner to complete the critical thinking exercise, "Identifying Uses of Authority," on p. 7 of the student text. The reading selection from Mark Twain's *Roughing It* describes a chain of events that occurred in the Old West when two men sought to avenge the assassination of their friend. Read the directions for completing the exercise with the class and review the questions in "Examining the Situation" on p. 8 of the student text. Ask students to share their responses with the class. Some possible responses students might give are included in the chart below.

PROBLEM	HOW MIGHT AUTHORITY BE USED TO SOLVE THE PROBLEM?
1. Violent arguments and fights (conflict)	1. Hire a law-enforcement officer
2. Possibility of injury lack of safety	2. Establish courts to try suspected lawbreakers
3. Property damage	3. Enact laws forbidding certain acts of violence
4. Citizens are afraid	4. See 1, 2, and 3
5. Basic rights are not protected	5. See 1, 2, and 3

Conclude this part of the lesson by asking students to identify contemporary problems that stem from an absence of effective authority. Students might suggest such problems as latch-key kids, vandalism, or gang violence. Encourage students to suggest ways that authority might help solve these problems.

D. Reading and Discussion
How can we use authority?

Have the class read "How can we use authority?" on p. 8 of the text. Ask students to identify ways we use authority to protect our rights to life, liberty, and property. Record their responses on the board. Their responses should include the following:

- **provide order and security**
- **manage conflict peacefully and fairly**
- **protect important rights and freedoms**
- **ensure that benefits and burdens are distributed fairly**

Ask students to cite examples from the reading or their experience that illustrate each use of authority.

E. Critical Thinking Exercise
Identifying Problems Related to Authority

Have the class work in groups of three students to complete the critical thinking exercise, "Identifying Problems Related to Authority," on p. 9 of the student text. The reading selection, "A Problem at Pacific Central High," describes how one school used authority to create an athletic program that included female students. Read the directions with the class and review the questions in "Examining the Situation" on p. 10. Ask students to share their responses with the class. Some responses students might give include the following:

1. **What problems occurred at Pacific Central High School several years ago?**

   Students should recall the following:

   - more money was spent on the boys' athletic program than on the girls' program (unfair distribution of resources)

   - girls never knew exactly when they could use the field (lack of predictability)

- since they had to practice after dark using second-rate equipment, some girls were injured unnecessarily (lack of safety)

2. **How was authority used to deal with these problems?**

   Students should recall that Congress passed legislation requiring schools that receive government money should provide both boys and girls equal opportunities in all school programs. The State Department of Education began checking to make sure that schools were obeying this new law.

3. **What problems at Pacific Central still have not been solved?**

   Students should recall the following:

   - the girls' basketball team only gets to use the gym twice a week

   - there is no gymnastics team for the girls who want to compete in this sport

   - girls' coaches do not get paid as much as boys' coaches

4a. **How might authority be used to deal with these problems?**

   Students should be encouraged to suggest and explain various possible solutions, such as the following:

   - school administrators should make sure that the athletic department's budget and facilities are allocated equally between boys' and girls' programs

   - state and federal officials should continue to check on school districts

   - female students and their coaches should file suits in court to force school officials to comply with the law

   - parents and community leaders should urge school administrators to rectify the situation

4b. How can you work to promote changes in a situation like this one?

Students might suggest the following:

- writing to the school board

- informing other students about the situation by writing in the school newspaper

- petitioning school administrators to ask for equal access

Help students think of examples in their school or community where young people have helped to solve problems when there was a lack of authority.

F. Concluding the Lesson

Direct attention to the illustrations on pp. 8 and 9 of the text. Ask students to respond to the captions:

- How can the absence of authority endanger lives, liberty, and property?

- How can authority be used to ensure fairness?

Have students re-read "Purpose of Lesson" on p. 7 of the text. Ask them to describe the extent to which they achieved the objectives of the lesson.

Using the Lesson

The activities suggested in "Using the Lesson" on p. 10 of the text reinforce or extend the information students learned about the use of authority. You may have the students work individually or in small groups to complete each of the suggested activities. Have students share their work with the class.

Lesson 3:   Where Is Authority Found and How Is It Justified?

Lesson Overview

Students learn that we find authority in certain **roles** (jobs or positions), **institutions, rules, laws, customs,** and **moral principles.** Students learn some common arguments used to justify the source of governmental authority, such as a right given by a supreme being or by the consent of the governed. Students also learn why it is important to identify and evaluate the **sources of authority** in certain situations. In a final critical thinking exercise, the class identifies and evaluates the sources of authority in the case *Regina v. Amah, Avinga, and Nangmalik.* The case raises an issue of conflicting sources of authority when Inuit (Eskimo) custom expects family members to aid in the suicide of an elderly relative, contrary to Canadian law.

Lesson Objectives

At the conclusion of this lesson, students should be able to do the following:

- identify some sources of authority

- explain why it is important to know the source of authority in certain situations

- evaluate a case using the ideas they have learned

Preparation/Materials Required

Student text pp. 11-14

Optional: Invite a community resource person, such as a judge or attorney, to the class

Teaching Procedures

A. Introducing the Lesson

Read the following quotation to the class:

> *"We will match your capacity to inflict suffering by our capacity to endure suffering. We will meet your physical force with soul force. Do to us what you will and we will still love you, but we cannot in all good conscience obey your unjust laws."*
> Dr. Martin Luther King, Jr.
> December 24, 1967

- Ask students to identify the source of authority Dr. King implies in this statement. The quotation refers to King's conscience, or personal principles of morality, as the source of authority.

Next read the quotation from the book, *The Once and Future King,* where Merlin, the magician, explains why Arthur has been made King:

> *"I was not allowed to tell you before, or since, but your father was, or will be, King Uther Pendragon. . . . I know all about your birth and parentage, and who gave you your real name. . . .*
>
> *In future it will be your glorious doom to take up the burden and to enjoy the nobility of your proper title: so now I shall crave the privilege of being the very first of your subjects to address you with it—as my dear liege lord, King Arthur."*
> *The Once and Future King.* White, T.H.
> New York: Medallion Books, 1966.

- Ask students to identify the source of King Arthur's authority that Merlin implies in the passage. Merlin says that Arthur is king because his father was king; he has inherited his authority.

- Ask students to identify someone they know who exercises authority. Record their responses on the board.

- Ask students to explain where they think that person gets his or her authority.

While you post the "Terms to Know" on the board, have students read "Purpose of Lesson" on p. 11 of the student text.

B. Reading and Discussion
Where is authority found?

Have the class read "Where is authority found?" on pp. 11-12 of the text. Ask students to identify where to find authority. Record their responses on the board. They should include the following:

- **roles** (jobs or positions)
- **institutions**
- **laws** and **rules**
- **customs**
- **principles of morality**

Ask students to offer examples from the reading or their experiences that illustrate sources of authority. Some examples students might suggest include the following:

- **roles:** a doctor has the authority to prescribe certain medicines for his or her patients
- **laws and rules:** obeying a law that requires children to be home by a certain time recognizes the authority of that law
- **customs:** "first come, first served" is a long-standing rule rooted in tradition
- **moral principles:** most students do not cheat on exams because they believe it is wrong to do so

Direct attention to the photograph on p. 11 of the text. Ask students to respond to the question in the caption, "What authority does Congress have?" Help students understand that Congress is an **institution**, established and limited by the Constitution, with authority to make certain laws that people must obey. Representatives to Congress fulfill **roles** that grant them particular privileges and obligations. Congress has the authority to make **laws** and **rules** that all of us are obligated to follow. Some students may be aware that Congress follows many **customs** or traditions, such as filling positions based on seniority. Debates in Congress frequently refer to **moral principles**—what members believe is right or wrong behavior.

Direct attention to the illustration on the left side of p. 12 of the text. Ask students to respond to the question in the caption, "Would you steal something if you thought you wouldn't get caught?" Help students understand that an individual's conscience and principles of morality are important sources of authority.

C. Critical Thinking Exercise
Finding Your Own Examples of Authority

Have students work in small groups or with a study partner to complete the critical thinking exercise, "Finding Your Own Examples of Authority," on p. 12 of the text. Ask students to share their work with the class.

D. Reading and Discussion
Where does authority come from?

Have the class read "Where does authority come from?" on pp. 12-13 of the text. Students learn that people and institutions derive a right to regulate or control our behavior from a source that usually can be traced back step by step. For example, the authority of a teacher to control the classroom derives through the principal who was hired by the superintendent. The superintendent was hired by a school board that owes its authority to laws made by the state legislature. The legislature derives its authority from the state constitution created by the consent of the people of that state.

Direct attention to the illustration on the right side of p. 12 of the text. Ask students to respond to the question in the caption, "Can you trace the sources of a teacher's authority?" Have students draw or sketch an illustration tracing the authority of the teacher to control his or her classroom. Have the students share their illustrations with the class.

E. Reading and Discussion
What arguments are made to justify the authority of rulers and governments?

Have the class read "What arguments are made to justify the authority of rulers and governments?" on p. 13 of the text. Post the following justifications for governmental authority on the board:

- right given by a supreme being (Pope)
- right inherited by birth (Queen of England)
- right justified by superior knowledge (a "philosopher king")
- right given by the consent of the governed (president of the United States)

Ask students to define each category. Help students identify contemporary or historical governments that justify their authority on the basis of one or more of these categories.

F. Reading and Discussion
Why is it important to know the source of authority?

Have the class read "Why is it important to know the source of authority?" on p. 13 of the text. Discuss why it is important to know the source of someone's authority. Help students understand that in a constitutional system the authority of government is limited. In the United States it is important to know if the Constitution gives Congress the authority to enact certain laws or if the president or the courts have the authority to act in a certain way. Also help students understand that some sources of authority are higher than others, e.g., federal laws supersede state laws.

G. Critical Thinking Exercise
Identifying Sources of Authority

Have the class work in groups of three to five students to complete the critical thinking exercise, "Identifying Sources of Authority," on p. 13 of the text. The reading selection is based on a Canadian case, *Regina v. Amah, Avinga, and Nangmalik*, in which the courts were asked to rule on conflicting sources of authority. Inuit (Eskimo) tradition dictates that certain family members assist older people in ending their own lives, contrary to Canadian law. Read the directions for completing the exercise with the class and review the questions in "Examining the Situation" on p. 14 of the text. Ask the students to share their responses with the class. If you want to provide additional information regarding this case, please see "Teacher References" at the end of this page.

H. Concluding the Lesson

To conclude this lesson, direct attention to question number 3 in "Examining the Situation" on p. 14 of the text. Discuss with the class how *Regina v. Amah* illustrates the importance of identifying different sources of authority.

Have students re-read "Purpose of Lesson" on p. 11 of the text. Ask them to describe the extent to which they achieved the objectives of the lesson.

Using the Lesson

The activities suggested in "Using the Lesson" on p. 14 of the text reinforce or extend what students have learned about sources of authority and the importance of understanding the sources of authority in particular situations. You may have students work individually or in small groups to complete the activities suggested.

This lesson concludes the study of Unit One, "What Is Authority?" Have students write a summary in their journals of what they have learned about authority and power without authority, and about the sources of authority. They may also record questions about authority they still have and/or would like to explore.

Optional Reinforcement and Enrichment Exercises

The *Regina v. Amah, Avinga, and Nangmalik* case provides an opportunity to engage the class in role-playing a simulated court hearing. The roles involved include attorneys for the state, attorneys for Amah, Avinga, and Nangmalik, and a panel of judges. For instructions on conducting a simulated court hearing, refer to p. 17 of this guide.

Invite someone in your community to the class who has experienced living in a different culture. Ask the resource person to discuss people or institutions that exercise authority in that culture.

Teacher References

Regina v. Amah, Avinga and Nangmalik is a 1963 case from the Canadian Arctic involving the Inuit people. After World War II traditional Inuit culture began to change as a result of increased contact with Western traditions and law. The Supreme Court of the Northwest Territories became the forum where traditional Inuit practices were often judged against Canadian laws.

While criminal cases in the United States are brought forth in the name of the people of the national or state government (e.g., *U.S. v. Bonanno*, or *State of Mississippi v. Brown*), Canadian criminal cases are prosecuted in the name of the Queen or King. Regina, in Latin, means queen. "Regina," in this case, is Queen Elizabeth II of England.

Unit Two: How Can We Evaluate Rules and Laws, and Candidates for Positions of Authority?

Introduce Unit Two: How Can We Evaluate Rules and Laws, and Candidates for Positions of Authority? By this point in the curriculum, students have learned that authority manifests itself in two basic forms:

- positions of authority, such as teachers, police officers, mayors, etc., who by virtue of their positions have authority over certain people
- rules, such as school rules, traffic laws, and acts of Congress.

Explain that because authority affects our lives in so many ways, it is important to acquire knowledge and skills for making informed, intelligent decisions about matters relating to rules and to people in authority.This unit helps students make informed and reasoned decisions about such matters. During instruction in this unit, students learn practical, step-by-step procedures useful in performing three important tasks:

- selecting people to fill positions of authority
- evaluating rules to determine their strengths, weaknesses, and need for change
- developing new rules to deal with particular problems

These procedures are called "intellectual tools." For a detailed description of intellectual tools, refer to p. 6 of this guide.

Direct attention to the illustration on p. 15 of the student text. Ask students to identify the positions of authority shown in the picture. Ask students to respond to the question in the caption, "How should we choose people for positions of authority?" Explain in studying this unit the class will learn two sets of intellectual tools, one to help select people for positions of authority, and the other to help evaluate rules.

Have the class read "Purpose of Unit" on p. 15 of the text. Ask students to list two things they expect to learn from studying this unit.

Lesson 4: How Should We Choose People for Positions of Authority?

Lesson Overview

Students learn to identify the requirements of a position of authority and the qualifications a person should possess to fill that position. Students learn a set of intellectual tools designed to help them both analyze the duties of the position and to decide if an individual is qualified to serve in that particular position. In an excerpt from Theodore Roosevelt's *Winning of the West*, students learn the characteristics that qualified Lewis and Clark to fulfill the responsibilities of leading an expedition to the West.

Lesson Objectives

At the conclusion of this lesson, students should be able to do the following:

- explain why it is important to select carefully people to fill positions of authority

- identify and explain the duties, powers, privileges, and limitations of a position of authority

- identify and explain the qualifications a person should have to fill a particular position of authority

Preparation/Materials Required

Student text pp. 16-19

A copy for each student of the intellectual tool chart for selecting people for positions of authority on p. 19 of the student text

Optional: invite a candidate for a position of authority in local or state government to the class

Teaching Procedures

A. Introducing the Lesson

Ask students if they have ever been a candidate for a **position of authority** or had the responsibility of choosing someone to fill a position of authority. For example, have they ever applied for a job or chosen someone to represent them in the student council or a club office? Have students discuss the **qualifications** needed to fulfill the positions of authority they identified. Explain that these and other considerations will be the subject of this lesson.

While you post the "Terms to Know" on the board, have students read "Purpose of Lesson" on p. 16 of the text.

B. Reading and Discussion
Why should we be careful in selecting people to fill positions of authority?

Have the class read "Why should we be careful in selecting people to fill positions of authority?" on p. 16 of the student text. Remind the class that people whose role or job gives them authority to regulate or control aspects of our lives influence us every day. Ask students why they think it is important that people be well qualified for such positions. Ask students to identify some basic qualifications a person should possess to fill successfully a position of authority. Students should identify such fundamentals as knowledge, skills, and talents (later in the lesson students will learn to identify other qualities). In concluding the discussion, remind students that while someone may be well qualified to be a police officer, that person may not make a good teacher, and vice versa.

C. Critical Thinking Exercise
Identifying Qualifications for Leadership

Have students work with a study partner or in groups of three to complete the critical thinking exercise, "Identifying Qualifications for Leadership," on pp. 16-17 of the text. The selection is a passage from Theodore Roosevelt's *Winning of the West* describing why Thomas Jefferson appointed Lewis and Clark to lead an expedition through the Louisiana Territory.

Read the directions for completing the exercise with the class and review the questions in "Examining the Situation" on p. 17 of the text.

During class discussion, ask students to identify the responsibilities of Lewis and Clark. Record their responses on the board. Then ask the students to infer the qualifications that Lewis and Clark must have had to enable them to fulfill each responsibility. Record these responses next to the corresponding responsibilities already posted on the board. For example, students might identify the responsibility of observing and recording details about plants and animals along the route. The qualifications required to fulfill this responsibility could reasonably include knowledge of botany and zoology or drawing ability.

Direct attention to the illustration on p. 17 of the text. Ask students to respond to the question in the caption, "Why might it be important to select qualified people for positions of authority?"

D. Reading and Discussion
How should we choose someone for a position of authority?

This section of the lesson introduces students to a set of intellectual tools useful in selecting candidates to fill positions of authority. First, students complete a three-step analysis of the following:

1. the **duties, powers, privileges,** and **limitations** of the position

2. the **qualifications** a person should have to fill the position

3. the **strengths** and **weaknesses** of each candidate

Then students finish with the following:

4. decide which candidate would best fill the position of authority and explain their reasons

If you have not already done so, explain the purpose and uses of intellectual tools to the class. You will find a detailed discussion of intellectual tools on p. 6 of this guide.

Have the class read "How should we choose someone for a position of authority?" on pp. 17-18 of the student text. Post each of the four steps in the intellectual tools on the board and review the considerations in each with the class.

After reviewing all the considerations, refer again to the selection on Lewis and Clark on p. 16 of the text. Encourage students to identify and/or infer that Lewis and Clark had the following duties, powers, and privileges:

- to lead an expedition safely across to the Pacific Ocean and back
- to discover and map a practical route to travel from the Mississippi River to the Pacific Ocean
- to record accurately observations of wildlife, plants, and geography
- to establish friendly relationships with native peoples, to record their languages, and to learn about the land and environment from them
- to maintain discipline and be responsible for the health, safety, and morale of members of their expedition

Students might infer that certain limitations were placed on the authority of Lewis and Clark. They could not do the following:

- deviate too far from the goal set by President Jefferson
- be unduly cruel or harsh to the members of their expedition
- antagonize or be disrespectful toward the Native Americans they encountered; their authority was limited where other authority already existed
- bring back furs or other goods for their own gain

You may want students to revisit the list of qualifications they originally inferred for Lewis and Clark. Encourage them to suggest additional qualifications.

E. Critical Thinking Exercise
Identifying Qualifications Required for a Position of Authority

Have the class work in groups of three students to complete the critical thinking exercise, "Identifying Qualifications Required for a Position of Authority," on p. 18 of the text. Read the directions for completing the exercise with the class. Distribute a copy to each student of the intellectual tool chart on p. 19 of the student text. Allow adequate time for students to complete their analysis of the position of student judge and to determine which qualifications a person should have to fill the position.

After the groups have completed their work, reconvene the class. Choose a student to chair a simulated meeting of the student council. He or she should call on group spokespersons to explain their ideas. The entire class should then create a composite list of qualifications for the position of student judge, referring once again to the list of duties, powers, privileges, and limitations of the position.

F. Concluding the Lesson

To conclude the lesson, discuss how the intellectual tools might help students fulfill their responsibilities as citizens of their school and community. For example, how might these tools help them select a person for chair of a school dance? How could they help voters decide for whom to vote in the next mayoral election?

Have students re-read "Purpose of Lesson" on p. 16 of the text. Ask them to describe the extent to which they achieved the objectives of the lesson.

Using the Lesson

The activities suggested in "Using the Lesson" on p. 18 of the student text reinforce or extend what students have learned about selecting a person for a position of authority. When completing each of the activities, encourage students to use the intellectual tools for selecting persons for positions of authority.

Optional Reinforcement and Enrichment Exercises

Consider inviting a person who holds a position of authority in local government to the class. In preparation for the visit, advise the resource person that students will be inquiring about the qualifications needed to fill his or her position, along with the duties, powers, privileges, and limitations of that position.

The Journals of Lewis and Clark. A Mentor Book, Penguin Viking, New York, 1969 reprinted 1993. The introduction by Dr. John Bakeless and selections from the journals provide fascinating material for discussion about the qualifications, characteristics, and duties of other members of the Lewis and Clark expedition. Students might be particularly interested in Sacajawea, the Shoshone guide, and York, the African-American member of the expedition, as well as the background of both Lewis and Clark.

Lesson 5: Who Should Be Selected for This Position of Authority?

Lesson Overview

Students apply the intellectual tools to analyze a position of authority and to evaluate and decide which person might best fill that position. During the lesson the class role-plays a television debate among candidates for mayor of Jeffersonville, an imaginary town. Students conduct an election to select the person best qualified for the position.

Lesson Objectives

At the conclusion of this lesson, students should be able to do the following:

- use the intellectual tools to analyze a position of authority and to evaluate the qualifications of the candidates for public office

- decide which candidate is most qualified for the position and explain the reasons for their choice

Preparation/Materials Required

Student text pp. 20-23

Optional: name cards for each of the four roles represented in the role-play activity and a ballot listing the three candidates for mayor

---

Teaching Procedures

A. Introducing the Lesson

While you post the "Terms to Know" on the board, have students read "Purpose of Lesson" on p. 20 of the text.

B. Critical Thinking Exercise
Choosing Candidates for Public Office

During this lesson, students role-play a television debate with the candidates for mayor of an imaginary city. Post the following four roles on the board:

- The Fair Politics League
- Robert "Bob" Burns
- Suzanne Winston
- Jamie Tsing

Have the class read "Choosing Candidates for Public Office" on p. 20 of the text. Review the process for participating in this role-playing activity. Discuss the information presented in the section, "Mayor for Jeffersonville," with the class. Ask students to identify the economic, social, and educational issues facing Jeffersonville. Record their responses on the board.

Ask students to identify the duties, powers, privileges, and limitations of the position of mayor. Record their responses on the board. Then ask the class to create a list of qualifications a person should have to do the job well. Again, record student responses on the board.

Assign students to four groups representing the four roles in this activity. Have the Fair Politics League read their role-play instructions on p. 21 of the text. Have the candidate groups read their instructions on p. 22 as well as the profile of their candidate. Check that students understand their responsibilities in preparing for the role-play. Finally, review the "Instructions for Conducting the Debate" on p. 23 of the text. Allow adequate time for students to prepare their roles before conducting the debate. For more detailed instructions on conducting a debate, refer to p. 22 of this guide.

Following the debate, conduct a mock election for mayor. Review the questions in "Reaching a Class Decision" on p. 23 of the text with the class. You may want to prepare ballots in advance of the activity.

C. Concluding the Lesson

Tally the ballots for the mock mayoral election and announce the results. Discuss whether or not the students think that the best person was elected mayor of Jeffersonville. Have them explain their positions.

Direct attention to the illustration on p. 22 of the text. Ask students to respond to the question in the caption, "How can a public debate help you select the best-qualified candidate?" Discuss how useful the intellectual tools were to the class in helping decide how to vote.

Lesson 6:   What Should Be Considered When Evaluating Rules?

Lesson Overview

This lesson introduces students to the intellectual tools for evaluating rules and laws. Students examine a series of rules to determine their weaknesses and to help them learn the **characteristics** of a good rule. Students then apply the intellectual tools for evaluating rules to decide whether to keep or change a new school board policy regarding school lockers.

Lesson Objectives

At the conclusion of this lesson, students should be able to do the following:

- identify the weakness in a rule

- explain the characteristics of a good rule

- apply the intellectual tools to evaluate and decide whether to keep or change a school rule

Preparation/Materials Required

Student text pp. 24-27

A copy for each student of the "Intellectual Tool Chart for Evaluating Rules and Laws" on p. 27 of the student text

Teaching Procedures

A. Introducing the Lesson

Introduce the lesson by announcing a new rule in your school. Post the rule on the board and invite students to express their opinions regarding the merits of the new rule. Some examples of a new rule might include the following:

- only students with brown eyes may play on the varsity soccer team
- Girls will receive As in this class; boys will receive Cs

Ask students to create a list of characteristics of a good rule. Record their responses on the board.

While you post the "Terms to Know" on the board, have students read "Purpose of Lesson" on p. 24 of the text.

B. Critical Thinking Exercise
Developing Criteria for Evaluating Rules

Have students work individually or with a study partner to complete the critical thinking exercise, "Developing Criteria for Evaluating Rules," on p. 24 of the text. Read the directions for completing the exercise with the class and review the questions in the "What do you think?" section. Ask students to share their responses with the class. Some responses students might offer appear in the chart on the next page. You may want to draw a similar chart to record student responses on the board.

Rule Number	Problem	A Good Rule Should...
1	The rule is unfair. It discriminates against people who have lived in Dry Gulch for less then five years.	Be fair
2	The rule is too difficult, if not impossible, to understand.	Be easy to understand
3	The rule is not likely to achieve the purpose it was designed for. While it may help the water department keep its accounts in order, it will not prevent people from wasting water.	Be well designed to achieve its purpose
4	The rule does not make clear what is expected. It does not specify what is meant by "too much" water.	Be clear or specific as to what is expected
5	The rule unnecessarily interferes with an important value, the people's right to privacy. The rule also makes it difficult for people to protect their personal property.	Be designed so that it does not interfere unnecessarily with other values, such as privacy or freedom
6	The rule is impossible to follow. Water is essential for survival.	Be possible to follow

C. Reading and Discussion
How can you decide what makes a good rule?

Have the class read "How can you decide what makes a good rule?" on p. 25 of the text.

Ask students to compare the **criteria** for a good rule the class listed earlier in the lesson with the characteristics described in the reading.

D. Critical Thinking Exercise
Evaluating Rules

Have students work in groups of three to five students to complete the critical thinking exercise, "Evaluating Rules," on p. 25 of the text. The reading selection, "The School Locker Debate," describes the reactions of the principal and students to a new school board rule: no lockers. Distribute a copy to each student of the "Intellectual Tool Chart for Evaluating Rules and Laws" on p. 27 of the student text. Provide time for students to complete this chart. Ask students to share their responses with the class.

E. Concluding the Lesson

With the class, discuss question number 6 in the intellectual tool chart, "Should the rule be kept as it is, changed, or eliminated? Why?" Encourage students to justify their positions on the issue by using the intellectual tools for evaluating rules.

Have students re-read "Purpose of Lesson" on p. 24 of the text. Ask them to describe the extent to which they achieved the objectives of the lesson.

Using the Lesson

The activities suggested in "Using the Lesson" on p. 26 of the text reinforce or extend what students learned about evaluating the characteristics of a good rule and using the intellectual tools for evaluating rules. You may have students work on these activities individually or in small groups. Have students share their work with the class.

Lesson 7: How Might You Evaluate and Improve a Law?

Lesson Overview

Students apply the procedures for evaluating rules and laws to the First Amendment to the United States Constitution. The critical thinking exercise is a role-play of a congressional hearing to develop and to debate alternative ways to write the First Amendment.

Lesson Objectives

At the conclusion of this lesson, students should be able to do the following:

- use the intellectual tools to evaluate a constitutional amendment

- create a constitutional amendment based on criteria for fair and reasonable laws

- take and defend a position on how the First Amendment might be written

- learn the significance of the First Amendment to the United States Constitution

Preparation/Materials Required

Student text pp. 28-30

Optional: Invite a community resource person, such as a teacher of political science or law, or a state or local politician, to the class to participate in the role-play activity with the students

Teaching Procedures

A. Introducing the Lesson

Explain that this lesson offers another opportunity for the class to use the intellectual tools for evaluating and using laws. Explain that during the lesson they will role-play a congressional debate.

While you post the "Terms to Know" on the board, have students read "Purpose of Lesson" on p. 28 of the text.

B. Reading and Discussion
What is the First Amendment?

Have the class read "What is the First Amendment?" on pp. 28-29 of the text. Discuss key information regarding the United States Constitution and the Bill of Rights with the class. Remind students that the Constitution is the supreme law of the land, superseding state constitutions and state laws. Remind students that the Constitution as ratified in 1787 did not contain a bill of rights. Review the negative experiences that the American colonists had with issues such as **free exercise of religion, freedom of speech, press, assembly,** and **freedom to petition for redress of grievances.** Help students understand that some people feared the reoccurrence of these experiences. They insisted on adding a bill of rights to the Constitution to protect their rights from violation by government officials who might use their authority unfairly.

You may want to invite a community resource person, such as a professor of law or political science, to the class to help students understand this material in more depth. The resource person also might help students prepare their roles for the congressional debate and participate in the concluding discussion.

C. Critical Thinking Exercise
Evaluating a Constitutional Amendment

Ask students to imagine themselves to be members of the first Congress of the United States. Explain that as members of Congress, they have a right to suggest amendments to the Constitution and to evaluate those suggested by others. Explain that some members have just proposed the amendment they are about to read. Have the class read the critical thinking exercise, "Evaluating a Constitutional Amendment," on p. 29 of the text. Have students work with a study partner to respond to the questions in the "Examining an Amendment" section. Remind students that these are the same questions used in the intellectual tools for evaluating rules and laws. Ask students to share their responses with the class.

D. Critical Thinking Exercise
Developing and Debating a Constitutional Amendment

Post the following topics on the board:

- **freedom of religion**
- **freedom of speech and of the press**
- **freedom to assemble and to petition the government**

With the class read the directions for completing the critical thinking exercise, "Developing and Debating a Constitutional Amendment," on pp. 29-30 of the text. Assign students to work in groups corresponding to the three topics you have written on the board. Allow adequate time for students to draft their proposed amendments. Remind the groups that their proposals should in some ways limit the authority of government so that it cannot unreasonably or unfairly limit people's freedom. At the same time, the proposal should give government enough authority to place fair and reasonable limitations on people's freedom in order to make society better for all.

After small groups have completed drafting their proposals, review with the whole class "Conducting a Congressional Debate" on p. 30 of the student text. Check that students understand each step in the procedures for role-playing a congressional debate. Select a chairperson to serve as Speaker of the House who will chair the proceedings. Allow adequate time for students to prepare their presentations before conducting the debate. For detailed instructions on conducting a congressional debate, refer to p. 14 of this guide.

E. Concluding the Lesson

At the conclusion of the congressional debate, ask students to vote on the amendments they have discussed. Ask students to explain why they voted for or against each proposal. Ask students to evaluate the usefulness of using the intellectual tools to evaluate rules and laws.

Have students re-read "Purpose of Lesson" on p. 28. Ask them to describe the extent to which they achieved the objectives of the lesson.

Using the Lesson

The activities suggested in "Using the Lesson" on p. 30 of the text reinforce or extend what students have learned about evaluating rules and laws. You may have students work on these activities individually or in small groups.

This lesson concludes the study of Unit Two, "How Can We Evaluate Rules and Laws, and Candidates for Positions of Authority?" Have students write a summary in their journals of what they learned about using intellectual tools to select persons for positions of authority and for evaluating rules and laws.

Optional Reinforcement and Enrichment Exercises

Have students find news articles about various bills before your state legislature or city council. Ask students to evaluate the proposed legislation in terms of the criteria for fair and reasonable rules and laws that they learned in this lesson.

Unit Three: What Are the Benefits and Costs of Using Authority?

Introduce **Unit Three: What are the Benefits and Costs of Using Authority?** Direct attention to the illustration on p. 31 of the student text. Have students identify who is using authority in each of the pictures. Ask students to respond to the question in the caption, "What might be some benefits (advantages) and costs (disadvantages) of using authority?"

Explain to the class that every authoritative role, institution, rule, law, custom, or tradition, as well as every exercise of authority, carries with it certain benefits and costs for individuals, groups, or society. An understanding of the benefits and costs of authority in general and in specific situations is essential in making intelligent decisions about the scope and limits of authority. Students will address the question of scope and limits in Unit Four.

Some benefits and costs of authority are inherent in the concept itself. For example, any exercise of authority necessarily entails a restriction upon individual freedom. Paradoxically, authority is essential for the existence of freedom.

Other benefits and costs of authority have become evident through human experience. For example, authority can provide a sense of security. On the other hand, subjects of authority must maintain a constant vigilance because of its potential for misuse.

Have the class read "Purpose of Unit" on p. 31 of the student text. Ask students to list three things they expect to learn from their study of Unit Three.

Lesson 8: What Are Some Consequences of Using Authority?

Lesson Overview

Students learn to identify the consequences of the use of authority. They analyze hypothetical situations, identify the possible consequences of the use of authority, and classify those consequences as benefits (advantages) or costs (disadvantages). Students then learn some of the most common benefits and costs of authority in our society. Finally, the class role-plays a state legislative hearing to consider the benefits and costs of a proposed law that encourages students to remain in high school until graduation.

Lesson Objectives

At the conclusion of this lesson, students should be able to do the following:

- identify possible consequences of using authority

- classify those consequences as benefits or costs

- weigh the benefits and costs to arrive at a position about the exercise of authority

Preparation/Materials Required

Student text pp. 32-36

Teaching Procedures

A. Introducing the Lesson

While you post the "Terms to Know" on the board, have students read "Purpose of Lesson" on p. 32 of the text.

B. Critical Thinking Exercise
Identifying and Classifying
Consequences of Authority

Have the class work in groups of three to five students to complete the critical thinking exercise, "Identifying and Classifying Consequences of Authority," on pp. 32-33 of the text. Read the directions for completing the exercise with the class and review the questions in the "What do you think?" section on p. 33. Assign one of the four situations described on p. 32 to each group. Ask each group to identify the possible consequences of the use of authority in that particular situation. Ask them to classify those consequences as benefits or costs. Ask students to share their responses with the class.

C. Critical Thinking Exercise
Examining Common Benefits
and Costs of Authority

Post the following benefits of authority on the board:

1. **security**

2. **fairness**

3. **freedom** and **other rights**

4. **efficiency**

5. **provision of essential services**

6. **improved quality of life**

Have the class read the "Benefits" section in the critical thinking exercise, "Examining Common Benefits and Costs of Authority," on pp. 33-34 of the text. Ask students to define each of the benefits and to describe the examples in the reading. Record their responses next to the corresponding terms on the board. Have students work with a study partner to write an example from their experience that illustrates each benefit.

Post the following costs of authority on the board:

1. **misuse of power**

2. **need for vigilance**

3. **inaccessibility**

4. **limitations on freedom and other rights**

5. **economic or financial costs**

Have the class read the "Costs" section on pp. 34-36 of the text. Ask students to define each of the costs and to describe the examples in the reading. Record their responses next to the corresponding terms on the board. Again, have students work with a study partner to write an example from their experience that illustrates each cost.

D. Reading and Discussion
Which benefits and costs are most important?

Have the class read "Which benefits and costs are most important?" on p. 36 of the text. Discuss the importance of deciding which consequences of the use of authority are most important when making decisions about laws or the acts of people in positions of authority. Remind the class that it is important to consider different points of view when examining benefits and costs of authority.

E. Critical Thinking Exercise
Considering Benefits and Costs in Taking Positions on Issues of Authority

During this critical thinking exercise the class will role-play a state legislative committee hearing on the consequences of a proposed law. Post the following five roles on the board:

- Committee to Protect Students' Rights
- Police Department
- Parent-Teacher Association
- Jobs for Youth Employment Agency
- members of the state legislature

Have the class read the critical thinking exercise, "Considering Benefits and Costs in Taking Positions on Issues of Authority," on p. 36 of the text. The reading selection describes a proposed bill that would require students to surrender their drivers' licenses if they drop out of school. Review the questions in "Questions to Consider" and assign students to each of the five roles you posted on the board. Allow adequate time for the groups to evaluate the proposed law and to develop positions on the issue before role-playing the hearing. For detailed instructions on conducting a legislative committee hearing, refer to p. 12 of this guide.

F. Concluding the Lesson

At the conclusion of the presentations, ask the students role-playing members of the state legislature to decide whether or not to recommend passage of the proposed bill. Have them share their recommendation with the class. Encourage students to support their positions using the arguments they heard during the presentations. Discuss why it is important for persons in positions of authority to consider different viewpoints concerning the exercise of authority.

Have students re-read "Purpose of Lesson" on p. 32 of the text. Ask students to describe the extent to which they achieved the objectives of the lesson.

Using the Lesson

The activities suggested in "Using the Lesson" on p. 36 of the text reinforce or extend what students learned about examining the consequences of the use of authority and classifying those consequences as benefits or costs. You may have students work on the activities individually or in small groups. Have students share their work with the class.

Lesson 9: How Would You Evaluate the Benefits and Costs of a School Dress Code?

> ### Lesson Overview
>
> Students are provided with a final opportunity to apply what they learned about identifying consequences of authority and classifying them as benefits or costs. The class role-plays a school board hearing to decide whether or not to adopt a policy requiring students to wear uniforms to school.
>
> ### Lesson Objectives
>
> At the conclusion of this lesson, students should be able to do the following:
>
> - identify the possible consequences of using authority in a particular situation
> - classify those consequences as benefits or costs
> - weigh the benefits and costs to arrive at a position about the exercise of authority
>
> ### Preparation/Materials Required
>
> Student text pp. 37-39
>
> Optional: Invite a community resource person, such as a school administrator or school board member, to participate in the activities of the lesson with the class

Teaching Procedures

A. Introducing the Lesson

Direct attention to the illustration on p. 37 of the student text. Ask students to respond to the question in the caption, "What might be the benefits and costs of a school dress code?" Discuss who in your school district might have authority to decide about a dress code for students. What is the source of their authority, and who might influence the exercise of authority in

that situation? Help students understand the role of the local school board and of citizens in policy decisions within your school district.

Have students read "Purpose of Lesson" on p. 37 of the text.

B. Reading and Discussion
The School Uniform Debate

Have students work with a study partner to read and discuss "The School Uniform Debate" on pp. 37-38 of the text. The selection describes a proposed school board policy requiring students to wear school uniforms to make school campuses safer and to improve student discipline. Review the questions in the "What do you think?" section on p. 38 with the class. Ask students to share their responses with the class.

C. Critical Thinking Exercise
Identifying and Weighing Benefits and Costs

The class role-plays a school board hearing on the proposed dress code for students. Post the following six roles on the board:

- School Board
- Students and Parents for School Uniforms
- Students and Parents for Free Choice
- Springville Teachers Union
- Protect Our Rights Association
- Association of Springville School Principals

Have the class read the critical thinking exercise, "Identifying and Weighing Benefits and Costs," on pp. 38-39 of the text. Assign students to the six roles you posted on the board. Check that the groups understand the steps in preparing to participate in the role-play activity. Allow adequate time for students to analyze the consequences of the proposed school board policy and to prepare their positions on the issue. If you have invited a community resource person to the class, ask him or her to assist the students in preparing their roles. You may want your resource person to join the group role-playing the school board.

Before conducting the school board hearing, review "Conducting the Hearing" on p. 39 of the text with the class. Check that students understand the procedures for participating in a simulated school board hearing.

For instructions on conducting a hearing, refer to p. 12 of this guide.

D. Concluding the Lesson

At the conclusion of the hearing, allow time for the members of the school board to reach a decision about the policy. Have the chairperson announce the decision and explain the reasoning supporting their choice. If any board member disagreed with the majority decision, allow that board member time to explain why he or she disagrees. Conduct a class discussion by asking students to respond to the questions in "Discussing the Hearing" on p. 39 of the text. If you have invited a community resource person to the class, ask him or her to participate in this concluding discussion and to share observations about how realistic the simulated hearing has been.

Have students re-read "Purpose of Lesson" on p. 37 of the text. Ask students to describe the extent to which they achieved the objectives of the lesson.

Using the Lesson

The activities suggested in "Using the Lesson" on p. 39 of the text reinforce or extend what students learned about identifying the consequences of the use of authority and classifying those consequences as benefits or costs. You may have students complete the activities individually or in small groups. Have students share their work with the class.

This lesson concludes the study of Unit Three, "What Are the Benefits and Costs of Using Authority?" Have students summarize in their journals what they learned about identifying the consequences of the use of authority and classifying them as benefits or costs.

Unit Four: What Should Be the Scope and Limits of Authority?

Introduce **Unit Four: What Should Be the Scope and Limits of Authority?** Explain that this unit focuses on one of the most important aspects of authority. If authority is to be used to fulfill the functions that students learned about in Unit Two and if it is to achieve the kinds of benefits discussed in Unit Three, then the position through which that authority is to be exercised must be provided with sufficient powers and resources. On the other hand, if the costs of authority introduced in Unit Three are to be avoided or minimized, then clear limits on that authority and mechanisms for enforcing those limits must be established.

This unit helps students understand and apply procedures and considerations useful in determining the scope and limits of authority. The terms **scope** and **limits** as used here refer to the set of duties, powers, privileges, and limitations assigned to a particular position of authority (e.g., law enforcement officer, judge, member of Congress) or an institution (e.g., a police department, the judiciary, the Congress). The procedures and considerations will be used to evaluate individual positions of authority and authoritative institutions and to design or create new positions and institutions.

Direct attention to the photographs of Nazi Germany on p. 40 of the student text. Ask students to identify some consequences that arose from the design of this position of authority. What was Hitler's position? How might they re-design this position of authority to avoid the recurrence of such a use of power?

Have the class read "Purpose of Unit" on p. 40 of the text. Ask student to list three things they expect to learn from their study of Unit Four.

Lesson 10: What Should You Consider in Evaluating a Position of Authority?

Lesson Overview

Students examine several hypothetical positions of authority and identify the weaknesses in the design of those positions. Based on the weaknesses identified, students develop a list of considerations useful in evaluating the strengths and weaknesses of any position of authority. The lesson also introduces a set of intellectual tools designed to help students evaluate and suggest possible improvements for positions of authority and institutions.

Lesson Objectives

At the conclusion of this lesson, students should be able to do the following:

- explain why positions of authority need to be properly designed

- identify the weaknesses in poorly designed positions of authority

- infer what the weaknesses suggest about a well-designed position of authority

- explain the intellectual tools used in evaluating and suggesting improvements for positions of authority

Preparation/Materials Required

Student text pp. 41-43

Teaching Procedures

A. Introducing the Lesson

Ask students to identify some ways in which people in positions of authority affect their lives. During the discussion, encourage students to consider parental and school authorities as well as government officials.

Ask students why it might be important for them to be able to evaluate positions of authority. Have the class read "Purpose of Lesson" on p. 41 of the text.

B. Reading and Discussion
Why is it important to be able to evaluate positions of authority?

Have the class read "Why is it important to be able to evaluate positions of authority?" on p. 41 of the student text. Help students understand that to preserve the freedom of our society we need to be able to evaluate how positions and institutions of authority are designed. Although people in positions of authority should be given enough power to do their jobs, we must place effective limits on their powers to protect our rights. Since we live in a constitutional democracy, we have the right to a voice in the establishment, perpetuation, or modification of many positions of authority on local, state, and federal levels. The exercise of this right is important because people who fill those positions of authority participate in activities that affect our everyday lives. A lack of attention to the design of these positions and the way people in the positions fulfill their duties can lead to consequences that may be minimal or quite significant. These consequences could include the loss of basic freedoms and the undermining of other principles and values on which our nation was founded.

C. Critical Thinking Exercise
Identifying Weaknesses in Positions of Authority

Have students work with a study partner to complete the critical thinking exercise, "Identifying Weaknesses in Positions of Authority," on pp. 41-42 of the text. Each of the situations described in the reading, "What's Wrong Here?" contains one or more weaknesses in the design of the position of authority. With the class read the directions for completing the exercise and review the questions in the "What do you think?" section on p. 42. At the conclusion, ask students to share their responses. On the board, record their answers to each of the questions.

Post the following heading on the board: "A well-designed position of authority should. . . ." Then refer students to each item in the list of weaknesses recorded on the board (question number 3 in "What do you think?"). Ask the class what each weakness suggests about a well-designed position of authority. Record their responses on the board. Some responses students might offer include the following:

A well-developed position of authority should

- not be overburdened with duties
- be designed with sufficient accountability
- be assigned appropriate power(s)
- be designed to allow public input
- provide enough resources to do the job
- require fair and humane procedures in the exercise of its authority
- be subject to periodic review

Based on their knowledge and experience, ask students to expand the list by offering additional thoughts about a well-designed position of authority. Their responses might include the following:

A well-developed position of authority should

- have clear limits on the power allocated to it
- be designed so that it will not interfere unnecessarily with important values, such as individual dignity, freedom of speech, privacy, etc.
- be adaptable to changing circumstances

Explain to the class that each of these considerations should be used whenever students evaluate a position of authority. Ask students to copy this list in their notebooks or journals for later use.

D. Reading and Discussion
How can you evaluate a position of authority?

Have the class read "How can you evaluate a position of authority?" on p. 42 of the text. This reading reviews the criteria for evaluating a position of authority that students developed during the previous critical thinking exercise. Help students understand that properly planned positions of authority give people in those roles enough power to carry out their assigned duties while placing clear limits on their powers. Review the questions they might use to consider the strengths and weaknesses of a position of authority discussed in the reading.

E. Concluding the Lesson

Read and review the "Intellectual Tool Chart for Evaluating Positions of Authority" on p. 43 of the student text with the class. Explain that they will apply these intellectual tools to evaluate and to make decisions about a position of authority described in the next lesson.

Using the Lesson

The activities suggested in "Using the Lesson" on p. 42 of the text reinforce or extend what students have learned about evaluating positions of authority. Encourage students to use the criteria they learned during the lesson in completing these exercises. You may have students work individually or in small groups to complete these activities. Have students share their work with the class.

Lesson 11: How Would You Improve This School Principal's Position?

Teaching Procedures

A. Introducing the Lesson

Have the class read "Purpose of Lesson" on p. 44 of the student text. Explain that during this lesson the class will use the intellectual tools to evaluate the duties, powers, privileges, and limitations of a high school principal in a hypothetical school district and to offer suggestions for improving the position.

B. Critical Thinking Exercise
Evaluating a Position of Authority

Have the class work in groups of three to five students to complete the critical thinking exercise, "Evaluating a Position of Authority," on pp. 44-45 of the text. The reading, "Midvale High School," describes the powers, duties, privileges, and limitations of a school principal. It also describes the problems that arose when the principal made a rule forbidding students to wear black armbands to protest the environmental destruction caused by the coal mines located near their community.

Read the directions for completing the exercise with the class and review the questions in the "What do you think?" section on p. 45 of the text. Make sure each student has a copy of the "Intellectual Tool Chart for Evaluating Positions of Authority" on p. 43 of the student text. Allow adequate time for students to evaluate the position of authority and to develop suggestions for improving the position.

C. Concluding the Lesson

After the groups have completed their work, ask the students to share their responses to the questions in the "Intellectual Tool Chart for Evaluating Positions of Authority." Some responses students might offer are on the chart on the next page.

Intellectual Tool Chart for Evaluating Positions of Authority

Questions	Answers
1. What position of authority is to be evaluated?	Midvale High School principal
2. What is the purpose of the position?	To supervise and provide leadership for the school.
3. Is the position necessary? Why or why not?	Students should express individual opinions about the necessity of the position.
4. What are the duties, powers, privileges, and limitations of the position?	See job description on p. 44 of the text.
5. What might be the consequences of this position as it is designed?	Note: Students have not been provided much information about the consequences of the position. They should think of possible consequences.
6. What are the weaknesses (if any) in the way the position is designed? ■ number of duties ■ resources provided ■ grant and limitation of power ■ accountability ■ controls to prevent misuse of authority ■ requirement of fair procedures and respect for important values	■ There is a lack of clear limits on power. For example, there are no clear limits on what the principal might choose to allow or prohibit in establishing dress and behavior codes. ■ The position seems overburdened with too many duties. ■ There is insufficient power to communicate directly with the community and explain actions. Though the principal is charged with the duty of community involvement, the school board must approve all bulletins—a difficult thing to do when the board is not in session. ■ The position is not designed with sufficient controls to make sure it does not interfere with important values such as the right of free expression.
7. What changes would you suggest to improve the position? What would be the benefits and costs of these changes? Why?	Students might suggest the following and should note the costs and benefits of their proposals: ■ Putting limits on the principal's power to interfere with students' rights of free expression and other important values. ■ Delegate the principal's duties to others when organizing a new school. ■ Remove the requirement that the principal must have the board approve community bulletins.
8. Do you think the position should be eliminated, left as it is, or changed? Explain your reasoning.	Students should write their final conclusions and one or two sentences justifying their positions.

Next, direct attention to question number 2 in the "What do you think?" section on p. 45 of the text, "What changes would you suggest to improve this position of authority?" Have each group select a person to write the group's suggestions on the board. Ask the class to examine the suggestions and decide whether or not they will correct the weaknesses in the position of authority.

Conclude the discussion by asking students to respond to question number 3 in the "What do you think?" section on p. 45 of the text, "How would you evaluate the principal's decision to forbid the wearing of armbands to school? Do you agree or disagree with the arguments he used to justify this rule? Why?"

Using the Lesson

The activities suggested in "Using the Lesson" on p. 45 of the text reinforce or extend what students have learned about evaluating positions of authority. Encourage students to use the criteria they learned during the lesson in completing these exercises. You may have students work individually or in small groups to complete these activities. Have students share their work with the class.

Optional Reinforcement and Enrichment Exercises

Conduct a simulated school board hearing. Have some students role-play parents and students who participated in the protest and others role-play those who are sympathetic with the actions taken by the principal. Each group should use the intellectual tools to analyze the problem and then develop a statement expressing the opinion of their group.

Invite your school attorney or another lawyer to discuss the case of *Tinker v. Des Moines* (see "Teacher References"). Be sure your guest is prepared to discuss the scope and limits of authority in these cases.

Invite the principal of your school to join the students as they review the job description of Midvale's high school principal. Have students interview the principal to determine the similarities and differences between the Midvale High School principal and his or her actual position.

Teacher References

Tinker v. Des Moines Independent Community School District, 393 U.S. 503 (1969).

A group of high school and junior high students in Des Moines planned to protest the Vietnam War by wearing black armbands to school. On learning of the plan, school officials adopted a policy forbidding the wearing of armbands. Three students wore armbands to school in violation of school policy. When they refused to remove them, they were suspended until they returned without the armbands. The students claimed that the action violated their First Amendment right to free expression.

The case was eventually appealed to the U.S. Supreme Court. In a 7-2 decision, the Court ruled that the wearing of the armbands was "closely akin to pure speech" and protected by the First Amendment. The school environment did imply limitations on the freedom of expression, but here the principals lacked the justification for imposing such limitations. The "undifferentiated fear" of disturbance in the minds of the authorities was insufficient. While student expression could be forbidden when it materially disrupted school work or school discipline, these students had undertaken "a silent, passive expression of opinion, unaccompanied by any disorder or disturbance." Justice Hugo Black dissented, writing that the majority opinion was encouraging students to defy their teachers and arguing that the wearing of armbands had, in fact, diverted other students' attention from their schoolwork.

Lesson 12: How Would You Evaluate the Supreme Court's Power of Judicial Review?

Lesson Overview

Students use the intellectual tools to evaluate some of the powers and limitations of the United States Supreme Court. Students learn about the function and judicial processes observed by the Court when exercising its power of **judicial review**. At the conclusion, students examine the landmark case *Brown v. Board of Education* to determine what changes, if any, they would make in the Supreme Court's powers or limitations.

Lesson Objectives

At the conclusion of the lesson, students should be able to do the following:

- explain the function, powers, limitations, and judicial processes of the United States Supreme Court

- analyze the power of judicial review and evaluate some of its strengths and weaknesses

- use the intellectual tools to decide what changes, if any, to suggest in the Court's powers and limitations

Preparation/Materials Required

Student text pp. 46-50

A copy for each student of the "Intellectual Tool Chart for Evaluating a Position of Authority" on p. 43 of the student text

Teaching Procedures

A. Introducing the Lesson

Direct attention to the photograph of the Supreme Court Justices on p. 47 of the text. Ask students if they can identify the justices in the photograph (Front row: John Paul Stevens, Byron R. White, Chief Justice William H. Rehnquist, Harry A. Blackmun, Sandra Day O'Connor. Back row: David Souter, Antonin Scalia, Anthony McLeod Kennedy, Clarence Thomas). Note that this is a photograph of the 1992-93 Court. Explain that Ruth Bader Ginsburg has joined the Court, replacing Byron White.

While you post the "Terms to Know" on the board, have students read "Purpose of Lesson" on p. 46 of the text.

B. Reading and Discussion
What does the Supreme Court do?
What is the power of judicial review?
What are some limits on the power of judicial review?

Have the class read "What does the Supreme Court do?" on p. 46, "What is the power of judicial review?" on pp. 46-47, and "What are some limits on the power of judicial review?" on pp. 47-48 of the student text. You may want to use the "jigsaw" approach by assigning one-third of the class to each reading selection. Ask each group to read the designated material and explain the information to the others in the class.

During the class discussion, ask each group to share the information they learned in the reading with the entire class. Interrupt the discussions as necessary to review and check for accuracy of presentation. Take care to ensure that students learn the vocabulary in each section of reading and that they understand the powers, duties, privileges, and limitations of the Supreme Court. You may want to have students refer to Article III of the United States Constitution to find other powers of the Court not mentioned in the reading. Students should understand that the power of judicial review is not mentioned in the Constitution, but is based on the argument that the Supreme Court must protect and enforce the Constitution and interpret the laws. To do so, the Court must have the power to declare invalid laws and actions of the government that do not comply with the Constitution's requirements. Remind the class that the Court does not have the physical power to enforce its decisions; nevertheless, Supreme Court decisions are regarded as law.

C. Critical Thinking Exercise
Examining Powers and Limitations of the Supreme Court

Have students work with a study partner to respond to the questions in the critical thinking exercise, "Examining Powers and Limitations of the Supreme Court," on p. 48 of the student text. Allow adequate time for students to formulate their responses, and then ask them to share their responses with the class.

D. Critical Thinking Exercise
Analyzing and Evaluating the Power of Judicial Review

Have the class complete the critical thinking exercise, "Analyzing and Evaluating the Power of Judicial Review," on pp. 48-49 of the student text. The reading, "*Brown v. Board of Education*," describes the facts, the key arguments, and the Court decision in this landmark case. The reading also describes the opposition in many states to implementing the decision handed down by the Court. You may want students to work with a study partner to complete this exercise.

With the class read the directions for completing the exercise and review the questions in the "What do you think?" section on p. 50 of the text. Allow adequate time for students to complete their work. At the conclusion, have student share their responses.

Have the class work in groups of three to five students to suggest what changes, if any, they might make in the Supreme Court's power of judicial review. Ask students to identify the weakness each change is designed to correct and to consider the costs and benefits of each change they recommend. Have each group select a spokesperson and a recorder to take notes. Allow adequate time for students to complete their work.

E. Concluding the Lesson

Have the spokesperson from each group post on the board the group's recommendations for changing the Supreme Court's power of judicial review. Ask each group to explain the weaknesses the proposals are designed to correct and the benefits and costs of the proposed changes. Some changes students might suggest include the following:

- limit the power of judicial review to certain kinds of cases

- expand the power of the court to enforce its decisions
- amend the Constitution so that the Court does not have the power of judicial review, that is, so that the Court cannot overrule the will of the majority
- provide Congress with the power to veto Supreme Court decisions
- provide for the election of Justices
- set fixed terms of office for the Justices

After the class has had an opportunity to review the proposals posted on the board and to probe the reasoning in various groups, ask students to respond to the following question: Would you make one or more of these changes? Why? Conclude the discussion by pointing out that in this lesson students have been evaluating an authoritative institution using the procedure they learned in previous lessons for evaluating a position of authority. Although the questions have been modified slightly to deal with an authoritative institution, the approach remains the same.

> ### Using the Lesson
>
> The activities suggested in "Using the Lesson" on p. 50 of the text reinforce or extend what students have learned about evaluating authoritative institutions. Encourage students to use the criteria they learned during the lesson in completing these exercises. You may have students work individually or in small groups to complete these activities. Have students share their work with the class.

Optional Reinforcement and Enrichment Exercises

Invite a community resource person, such as an attorney or judge, to the class. Have the resource person help students analyze the Supreme Court case used in this lesson. Ask the resource person to explain the powers and limitations of the United States Supreme Court and to discuss how an issue reaches the Court and the procedures used to decide cases.

Lesson 13: How Would You Create a Position of Authority?

Lesson Overview

This is the culminating lesson in the study of authority. Students design a position of authority using the knowledge and skills acquired in previous lessons. Students role-play members of a special city council committee convened to create a position of authority in city government to deal with a number of environmental problems. During a simulated city council meeting, students present their proposals on what duties, powers, privileges, and limitations they recommend the position should have to deal effectively with the problem.

Lesson Objectives

At the conclusion of this lesson, students should be able to do the following:

- analyze a problem resulting from a lack of authority

- use the intellectual tools to design a position of authority

- evaluate the strengths and weaknesses of the duties, powers, privileges, and limitations recommended for a position of authority

- evaluate the effects, benefits, and costs of the position of authority as proposed

Preparation/Materials Required

Student text pp. 51-54

A copy for each student of the "Intellectual Tool Chart for Designing Positions of Authority" on p. 54 of the student text

Flip chart paper and markers for student presentations

Teaching Procedures

A. Introducing the Lesson

Direct attention to the illustration on p. 51 of the student text. Ask students to respond to the question in the caption, "How would you design a position of authority to deal with environmental problems?" Explain that in this lesson they will have an opportunity to design a position of authority by role-playing members of a special committee of the Rivertown City Council.

Have the class read "Purpose of Lesson" on p. 51 of the text.

B. Critical Thinking Exercise
Designing a Position of Authority

Direct attention to the critical thinking exercise, "Designing a Position of Authority," on p. 51 of the text. Ask students to read the selection "Cleaning Up the Environment." The reading describes the concerns residents of Rivertown have about protecting their environment and improving the quality of life in their community. After a series of public hearings, the city council decided to create a position of authority in city government to deal with environmental matters.

When the class has completed the reading, review the various environmental issues of concern to the residents of Rivertown. Help students understand the positions of state agencies, environmental and health experts, trade unions, and local businesses. Also review the options that the city council has considered regarding what kind of position of authority they might want to create.

Have the class work in groups of three to five students to do the following:

- analyze the problems in Rivertown
- decide what kind of position they want to create
- recommend what powers, duties, privileges, and limitations the position of authority should have

With the class read the directions for completing this phase of the activity, "Directions for the Committee," on p. 53 of the text. Make sure each student has a copy of the "Intellectual Tool Chart for Designing Positions of Authority" on p. 54 of the text. Allow adequate time for the groups to complete their work.

With the class read the directions for preparing the oral presentations, "Presenting Your Plan," on p. 53 of the text. Distribute flip chart paper and markers to each group and ask students to post the group's recommendations that they want to present to the class. Allow adequate time for students to prepare their presentations.

C. Concluding the Lesson

Select five students to role-play the city council. Have the groups present their plans to this panel following the instructions in "Presenting Your Plan." Encourage students to have everyone in their group speak and answer questions during the simulation. Presentations should include the three parts identified in the text:

- statement of purpose of the position
- recommended duties, powers, privileges, and limitations
- probable effects of the position as it has been planned

For more detailed instructions on conducting a simulated city council hearing, refer to p. 12 of this guide.

At the conclusion of the presentations, take a vote on which position of authority seems best designed to deal with the environmental issues confronting the Rivertown City Council. Discuss the strengths and weaknesses of the oral presentations with the class.

Using the Lesson

The activities suggested in "Using the Lesson" on p. 53 of the text reinforce or extend what students have learned about creating positions of authority. Encourage students to use the intellectual tools they learned during the lesson in completing these exercises. You may have students work individually or in small groups to complete these activities. Have students share their work with the class.

This lesson concludes the study of Unit Four, "What Should Be the Scope and Limits of Authority?" Have students summarize in their journals what they have learned about using intellectual tools both to evaluate positions of authority and institutions and to create positions of authority.

Optional Reinforcement and Enrichment Exercises

Invite a member of your city council or an environmental expert to participate in this final activity. Ask the resource person to serve as the chairperson of the city council. In addition to participating in the simulation, students might interview the resource person about his or her job and how it is designed. The resource person should discuss the considerations used when designing, selecting, or recommending a person to fulfill a position of authority.

Attend a city council meeting. Ask students to compare the session with the one they simulated in the class.

Concluding the Authority Curriculum

This concludes the study of the Authority curriculum. It will be valuable to both you and your students to reflect on and evaluate the total experience with this section of *Foundations of Democracy,* including the content and instruction methods. To each student distribute the chart, "Reflecting on Your Experience," on p. 28 of this guide. Remind students that they should not only reflect on and evaluate their experiences, but also those of the class. Have students share their responses with the class.

The Privacy Curriculum

Introduce the Privacy curriculum. Explain to students that the value American society places on privacy is reflected in the guarantees of the right to privacy provided in the Constitution, such as the Fourth Amendment's protection against unreasonable searches and seizures. The scope of these Constitutional protections has led some people to criticize that governmental agencies may not be able to gather information necessary for the enforcement of the law. Others disagree. They are fearful that the right to privacy is in great danger because of lawful and unlawful efforts by individuals and groups to gain information about citizens—efforts often enhanced by increasingly sophisticated technology. This debate about the proper scope and limits of the right to privacy is inevitable and likely to continue. Explain that during their study of this curriculum, students will examine the concept of privacy, its differences among individuals and cultures, its benefits and costs, and its proper scope and limits.

Have students read the "Introduction" on p. 56 of the student text. Discuss the following questions with the class:

- What do you think privacy is? What are some examples of privacy?
- Note the absence of the word "privacy" in the Fourth Amendment to the Constitution. In what ways does the amendment imply that citizens have a right to privacy? In what ways does it require that the government respect the right to privacy?
- In what ways might privacy be related to human freedom and dignity? In what ways might it be related to other important rights such as property and freedom of thought, expression, and religion?
- What limits might exist on citizens' rights to privacy? Why might such limits be necessary?

Conclude the discussion by asking students to offer reasons it might be important to study about privacy.

Unit One: What Is the Importance of Privacy?

Introduce Unit One: What Is the Importance of Privacy? Explain that this unit will help develop an understanding of privacy. Students will learn a definition of privacy and learn to identify and describe examples of privacy in a range of situations. Students also will learn to identify common ways people behave to restrict access to objects of privacy, such as maintaining secrecy and confidential relationships. Finally, they will learn the reasons organizations and institutions might need to maintain privacy or secrecy.

Direct attention to the illustration on p. 57 of the student text. Ask students to respond to the question in the caption, "Why is privacy important?"

Have the class read "Purpose of Unit" on p. 57. Ask students to list three things they expect to learn from their study of Unit One. If students are keeping a journal during their study of this curriculum, they can record this in their journals. These journal notations should be reviewed at the conclusion of the study of privacy. This activity should be repeated during the introductions to Units Two, Three, and Four.

Lesson 1:   What Is Privacy?

Lesson Overview

Students learn to identify and describe examples of privacy. Students read and discuss the definition of **privacy** and examine the types of objects people might want to keep private: facts, actions, places and possessions, thoughts and feelings, and communications. During the critical thinking exercise, students determine whether or not privacy exists in specific situations. They identify the **objects of privacy** and explain why someone might want to maintain privacy in each situation.

Lesson Objectives

At the conclusion of this lesson, students should be able to do the following:

- define the term **privacy**
- describe common objects of privacy
- distinguish between situations in which privacy does and does not exist
- explain why people may wish to maintain privacy in specific situations

Preparation/Materials Required

Student text pp. 56-59

Newspapers and/or newsmagazines, at least one for each group of three to four students

Optional: A copy for each student of the enrichment activity handouts: "What can poems, songs, and essays teach us about privacy?" and "Privacy Circle."

Teaching Procedures

A. Introducing the Lesson

Introduce the lesson by directing attention to the illustration on p. 58 of the student text. Ask students to respond to the question in the caption, "Why do people need privacy?" Record their responses on the board.

Have the class create a list of items that students might wish to keep private at school or at home. Record their responses on the board. Leave this list on the board to use when defining objects of privacy in the next section of the lesson, "What is privacy?"

While you post the "Terms to Know" on the board, have students read "Purpose of Lesson" on p. 58 of the text.

B. Reading and Discussion
What is privacy?

Have students read "What is privacy?" on p. 58 of the student text. Ask students to describe the term **privacy**. Record their responses on the board. Be sure that their definition includes the following:

- the right to decide whether information will be shared with others
- the right to **solitude**—the state of being alone, away from other people
- the right to be free from the interference of others

Ask students to describe the term **object of privacy**. List the five categories of objects of privacy on the board:

- facts
- actions
- places and possessions
- thoughts and feelings
- communications

Return to the list of private items on the board that the class created during the introduction to the lesson. Have them organize the items on that list according to the five categories for objects of privacy.

C. Critical Thinking Exercise
Identifying and Examining
Situations Involving Privacy

Divide the class into groups of three students. With the class, read the directions for completing the critical thinking exercise, "Identifying and Examining Situations Involving Privacy," on p. 58 of the text. Ask the groups to record their responses on a separate sheet of paper.

Have the groups share their responses with the class. Items number 1, 2, 4, 6, and 7 are examples of privacy; items number 3 and 5 are not. Item number 4 shows that privacy can exist even in the presence of others. Item number 5 shows that being apart from others is not always the same thing as having privacy; this point may be underscored by comparing and contrasting items number 2 and 5.

D. Concluding the Lesson

Ask students to suggest examples of privacy from books, television, films, or the news. Students should explain the following:

- who was keeping something private
- the object of privacy
- from whom it was being kept private

Ask students to think of reasons these objects might be kept private.

Divide the class into groups of three to five students. Give each group a newspaper and/or newsmagazine and ask them to locate articles or stories that raise an issue of privacy. Ask students to identify who in the article or story is keeping something private, the object of privacy, and from whom it is being kept private. Ask students to offer reasons people keep these objects private. Have students share their articles and stories with the class. You may want students to use these materials to initiate a bulletin board on the topic of privacy.

Have students re-read "Purpose of Lesson" on p. 58 of the text. Ask them to describe the extent to which they achieved the objectives of the lesson.

Using the Lesson

The activities suggested in "Using the Lesson" on p. 59 of the text reinforce or extend what students have learned about identifying common objects of privacy and why people may wish to have privacy in specific situations. When working on any of the activities suggested, encourage students to refer to the five questions used in the critical thinking exercise:

1. **Why** is the situation an example of privacy?
2. **Who** wants to keep something private?
3. What is the **object of privacy**?
4. From **whom** is something being kept private?
5. **Why** do you suppose the person wants privacy?

You may want students to work on these activities individually or in small groups. Have students share their work with the class.

Collecting news clippings, as suggested in activity number 2, can be used to initiate a bulletin board project for the class. Students can be encouraged to contribute newspaper and magazine articles during the next few weeks of instruction.

Optional Reinforcement and Enrichment Exercises

These enrichment exercises require student handouts which should be copied and distributed to each student. The first activity concerns poems, song lyrics, and an essay that deal with privacy. Students identify the advantages and disadvantages of privacy that these writings suggest. They then answer the questions on the handout, "What can poems, songs and essays teach us about privacy?"

The second activity, the Privacy Circle, provides students with the opportunity to think about their personal privacy and the kinds of things people keep most private.

What can poems, songs, and essays teach us about privacy?

Poems, song lyrics, essays and other writings are often fun to read. They can make us think in new ways, or make us more aware of our own thoughts and feelings. As you read the following selections, think about the author's point of view. What is the author trying to tell us about privacy? Be prepared to share your thoughts with your class.

1. From *Something So Right*

   They got a wall in China–
   It's a thousand miles long.
   To keep out the foreigners they
     made it strong.
   And I got a wall around me
   That you can't even see.
   It took a little time to get next to me.

   by Paul Simon (American songwriter, 1942-)
   Copyright 1973 Paul Simon. Used by permission of the publisher.

2. From *Mending Wall*

   Before I built a wall I'd ask to know
   What I was walling in or walling out,
   And to whom I was like to give offense.
   Something there is that doesn't love a wall,
   That wants it down.

   by Robert Frost (American poet, 1874-1963)

3. From *Childe Harold's Pilgrimage*

   There is a pleasure in the pathless woods,
   There is a rapture on the lonely shore,
   There is society where none intrudes,
   By the deep Sea, and music in its roar:
   I love not Man the less, but Nature more,
   From these our interviews, in which I steal
   From all I may be or have been before,
   To mingle with the Universe, and feel
   What I can ne'er express, yet cannot
   all conceal.

   by Lord Byron (English poet, 1788-1824)

4. From *Walden*

   My nearest neighbor is a mile distant, and no house is visible from any place but the hilltops within half a mile of my own. I have my horizon bounded by woods all to myself; a distant view of the railroad where it touches the pond on the one hand, and of the fence which skirts the woodland road on the other. But for the most part it is as solitary where I live as on the prairies. I have, as it were, my own sun and moon and stars, and a little world all to myself.

   Men frequently say to me, "I should think you feel lonesome down there, and want to be nearer to folks, rainy and snowy days and nights especially." [But]I find it wholesome to be alone the greater part of the time. To be in company, even with the best, is soon wearisome and dissipating. I love to be alone. I never found the companion that was so companionable as solitude.

   Society is commonly too cheap. We meet at very short intervals, not having had time to acquire any new value for each other. We meet at the post-office, and at the sociable, and about the fireside every night; we live thick and are in each other's way, and stumble over one another, and I think that we thus lose some respect for one another.

   by Henry David Thoreau (American essayist, 1817-1862)

What do you think?

1. What does Paul Simon think about the invisible "walls" around people? What purpose do they serve? What problems or disadvantages do they cause?

2. What does Robert Frost think the disadvantages are of "building walls"? What do you think the disadvantages are? What are the benefits?

3. Do you ever try to keep a "wall" around you? When? What do you gain? What do you lose? Do you think you should try to keep a "wall" around you more often? Less often? Why?

4. What does Lord Byron think are the advantages of being alone? What does Henry Thoreau think? What do you think the advantages are? What are the disadvantages?

5. Do you ever want to be alone? When? How do you feel when you want to be alone, but you can't?

6. Can you feel lonely even when you are around other people? What is the difference between being alone and being lonely?

Privacy Circle Exercise

Most people will share some information about themselves with just about anyone. Other information they keep to themselves, or share only with close friends or family. Similarly, people do not mind doing some things in public while they will do other things only in private or with people they know and trust.

In the Privacy Circle Exercise students examine their needs for privacy.

1. Pass out a copy of the Privacy Circle Exercise Sheet to each student.

   ■ Ask students to record in circle "A" the kind of information about themselves they would be willing to share with strangers, e.g., librarians, store clerks, someone they meet on a bus.

   ■ Ask them to record in circle "B" the kind of information they would be willing to share with acquaintances, e.g., clergy, classmates, and neighbors.

   ■ Ask them to record in circle "C" the kind of information they would be willing to share with close friends and relatives.

   ■ Since inner circle "D" is reserved for oneself, ask students to make a "mental list" of the kind of information they are not willing to share with others.

2. Ask students to examine their sheets (and mental lists) to determine

   ■ why they felt they were willing to share or unwilling to share certain information in specific situations

   ■ if they discovered anything new about their needs for privacy

   ■ if they were surprised by anything they discovered

   ■ if they can make generalizations about their needs for privacy

3. Divide the class into groups of three or five. Ask students to discuss their responses in the various circles. Each group should choose a spokesperson to give a summary of the group's discussion to the entire class.

   Ask the spokesperson of each group:

   ■ What kinds of information were people in your group willing to share with strangers? With acquaintances? With friends? Not at all?

4. Then the class as a whole should discuss the following questions:

   ■ What were the similarities in everyone's lists?

   ■ What are the common characteristics of the information and activities people keep most private?

   ■ How would you feel if the information and activities you keep most private were broadcast on the TV news?

   ■ How would you feel if you could not share private information with your closest friends or relatives? How would it affect your relationships with them?

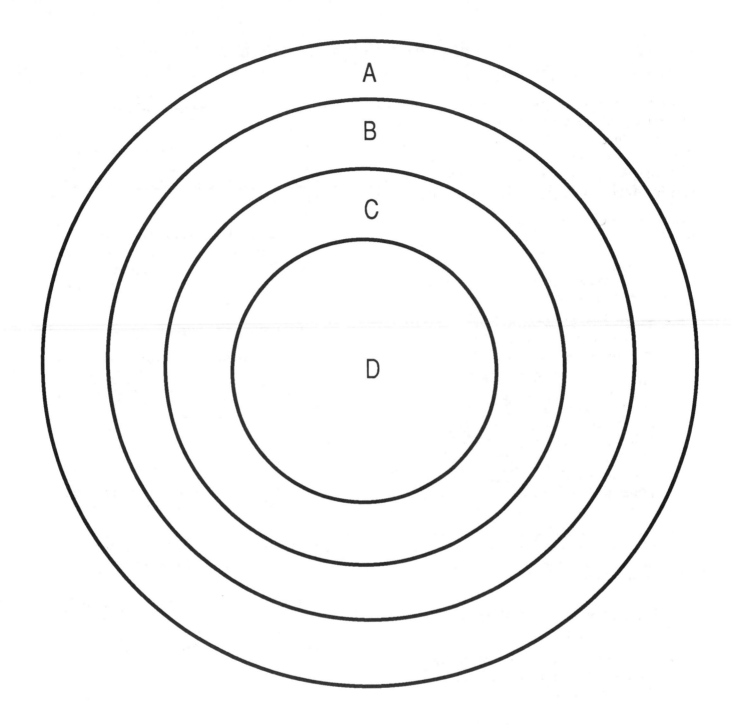

Privacy Circle

Circle A – List the kind of information about yourself you would be willing to share with strangers.

Circle B – List the kind of information you would be willing to share with acquaintances.

Circle C – List the kind of information you would be willing to share with close friends and relatives.

Circle D – Reserved for yourself; make a mental list of the kind of information you are not willing to share with others.

Lesson 2: How Do People Maintain Their Privacy?

Lesson Overview

This lesson broadens students' understanding of privacy by directing attention to several common ways that people behave to restrict the access of others to objects of privacy. These behaviors include the following:

1. isolating oneself
2. maintaining secrecy
3. establishing and maintaining confidential relationships
4. excluding others

During the critical thinking exercise students identify and analyze common ways of maintaining privacy or secrecy by examining a passage from Mark Twain's *Adventures of Tom Sawyer*. During the role-play activity, students decide whether or not Tom and Huckleberry Finn should reveal information concerning events they have secretly witnessed.

Lesson Objectives

At the conclusion of this lesson, students should be able to do the following:

- define the terms **isolation, secrecy, confidentiality,** and **exclusion**
- explain some common ways people behave to keep others from observing or finding out about objects of privacy or secrecy

Preparation/Materials Required

Student text pp. 60-63

A copy for each student of the "Chart for Identifying the Means Used to Maintain Privacy" on p. 71 of this guide

Teaching Procedures

A. Introducing the Lesson

Explain that people behave in different ways to keep things private from other people. Ask the class to offer some examples of common ways students behave to protect their privacy or secrecy at home and at school. Record their responses on the board. Leave this list on the board to use when defining "How do people behave to keep things private?" in the next section of the lesson.

While you post the "Terms to Know" on the board, have students read "Purpose of Lesson" on p. 60 of the student text.

B. Reading and Discussion
How do people behave to keep things private?

Have students read "How do people behave to keep things private?" on p. 60 of the student text. Ask the class to identify the four common ways that people behave to protect their privacy:

- isolation
- secrecy
- confidentiality
- exclusion

Record their responses on the board. Ask students to offer specific examples of each of these common behaviors. Remind students that people behave in different ways to keep things private from other people. Be sure students understand the relationship between privacy and secrecy. Explain that keeping a secret is one way to have privacy.

- One person can keep something secret to himself or herself.
- Two people can share a secret.
- Secrets can be shared by people who have a close personal relationship, such as parents and children, or friends.

When people who have a professional relationship, such as a doctor and patient or lawyer and client, share secrets, it is an example of confidentiality.

Return to the list that the class created during the introduction to the lesson. Have students organize the items on that list according to the four common behaviors they have just learned. Record their responses on the board.

C. Critical Thinking Exercise
Identifying the Means Used to Maintain Privacy

Have students work with a study partner to complete the critical thinking exercise, "Identifying the Means Used to Maintain Privacy," on p. 61 of the text. The reading selection is an excerpt from *The Adventures of Tom Sawyer* that describes Tom and Huck's behavior after secretly witnessing a crime. With the class, read the directions for completing the exercise. To each student, distribute a copy of the "Chart for Identifying the Means Used to Maintain Privacy" on p. 71 of this guide. After completing the chart, have students share their answers with the class. Possible answers are on the chart on the next page.

Have students return to work with their study partners. Assign one study partner in each pair to play the role of Huckleberry Finn and the other to play the role of Tom Sawyer. Ask the students to review the story. Huckleberry Finn should develop arguments to support the position that he and Tom should not reveal what they know about the events they secretly witnessed. Tom Sawyer should develop arguments to support the position that he and Huck should tell what they know about who committed the crime. Have students share their arguments with the class. Discuss the strengths and weaknesses of the arguments presented.

D. Concluding the Lesson

To conclude the lesson, have students write an ending to this episode in *The Adventures of Tom Sawyer*. Instruct them to include a brief description in their story of each character's privacy behavior using the terms **isolation**, **secrecy**, **confidentiality**, and **exclusion**. If students are keeping journals, this assignment can be written there. Have students share their ideas with the class for ending this episode in the story.

Have students re-read "Purpose of Lesson" on p. 60 of the text. Ask them to describe the extent to which they achieved the objectives of the lesson.

Using the Lesson

The activities suggested in "Using the Lesson" on p. 63 of the text reinforce or extend what students have learned about people's privacy behavior. When working on any of the activities suggested, encourage students to use the terms **isolation**, **secrecy**, **confidentiality**, and **exclusion**. You may have students work on these activities individually or in small groups. Have students share their work with the class.

Protecting confidential communications, as suggested in activity number 2, might be assigned as a role-play in which students create the roles of doctor/patient, lawyer/client, and teacher/student. Each party to the role-play develops a list of items that should remain confidential in the relationship (e.g., What do you learn in your job that should be kept private or secret? When you go to the doctor, what information do you believe that he or she should keep private?).

Asking Tom Sawyer to decide whether or not to violate his oath to Huck Finn, as suggested in activity number 3, presents students with a common moral dilemma, to tell or not to tell. In deciding what to do, Tom must balance the boys' personal safety and their contractual obligation to one another with their responsibility to the community, the law, and justice. Students can write what they think Tom should do in their journals. Have them share their ideas with the class.

Chart for Identifying the Means Used to Maintain Privacy

Who wished to keep something private or secret?	What did they wish to keep secret?	From whom did they wish to keep something secret?	How did they behave to maintain privacy or keep secrets?	Is it an example of isolation, secrecy, confidentiality, or exclusion?
Dr. Robinson	grave robbing	the authorities	worked in the dark of night	secrecy, exclusion
Muff Potter	the stabbing of Dr. Robinson	the authorities	kept quiet	secrecy
Joe	that he has an old score to settle with Dr. Robinson	Dr. Robinson	kept quiet until after they dug up William's body	secrecy
	who actually stabbed Dr. Robinson	Muff and the authorities	tricked Muff into thinking he killed the doctor	secrecy
Tom and Huck	that they were observing the grave digging	Dr. Robinson, Muff, and Joe	hid behind a tree	isolation, secrecy
	that they observed the scuffle	Dr. Robinson, Muff, and Joe	fled to the tannery	isolation
	who actually stabbed Dr. Robinson	the authorities	swore to keep "mum"; signed a pact in blood	secrecy, confidentiality
	the shingle on which they wrote their pact	everyone	buried it close to a wall	exclusion

Chart for Identifying the Means Used to Maintain Privacy

Who wished to keep something private or secret?	What did they wish to keep secret?	From whom did they wish to keep something secret?	How did they behave to maintain privacy or keep secrets?	Is it an example of isolation, secrecy, confidentiality, or exclusion?
Dr. Robinson				
Muff Potter				
Joe				
Tom and Huck				

Lesson 3: Why Might Institutions Need to Maintain Secrecy?

Lesson Overview

Students are introduced to the notion of institutional secrecy. Institutional secrecy is the practice by organizations and **institutions,** such as private corporations or government agencies, of keeping certain information secret to protect the interests of the institution. During the critical thinking exercise, students encounter an issue of institutional secrecy when a ninth-grade nominating committee requests access to the school records of six students they are considering for a special award.

Lesson Objectives

At the conclusion of this lesson, students should be able to do the following:

- describe the term **institution**
- explain why various private and public organizations or institutions may wish to keep things secret

Preparation/Materials Required

Student text pp. 64-66
Drawing paper and markers
Newspapers and/or newsmagazines

Teaching Procedures

A. Introducing the Lesson

Explain that individuals are not the only ones who need privacy, but that organizations and institutions, such as private corporations, political parties, government agencies, and even schools, often have things they want to keep private.

Direct attention to the illustration on p. 65 of the student text. Ask students to respond to the question in the caption, "Why might schools need to keep certain records private?" Record their responses on the board.

While you post the "Term to Know" on the board, have students read "Purpose of Lesson" on p. 64 of the text.

B. Reading and Discussion
What is an institution?

Have students read "What is an institution?" on p. 64 of the student text. Post a list on the board of the institutions referred to in the text:

- schools and universities
- business corporations
- museums
- hospitals
- federal, state, and local governments

Ask students to offer examples of objects that these institutions might want to keep private or secret. From whom might they want to keep them private or secret? Ask students to determine what might motivate institutions to keep these objects private or secret. In what ways might these institutions behave to keep these objects private or secret?

Have the students find newspaper and magazine articles that illustrate institutional privacy or secrecy. Ask them to share their articles with the class and then add the articles to a privacy bulletin board.

C. Critical Thinking Exercise
Examining Institutional Secrecy

Have the class work in groups of three to five students to complete the critical thinking exercise, "Examining Institutional Secrecy," on p. 64 of the student text. Read the directions with the class. Ask the groups to share their responses with the class to the questions on pp. 65-66 of the text.

Ask students to offer examples of other things a school might want to keep private. The students might suggest the addresses and phone numbers of teachers, the location of the security system, budget information, etc.

D. Concluding the Lesson

Distribute drawing paper and markers to the class. Ask students to create a drawing or cartoon illustrating something an institution wants to keep private or secret. Student drawings or cartoons should include the following:

- the object of privacy or secrecy
- from whom it is being kept private or secret
- how the object is being kept private or secret

Ask students to write a caption for their illustration explaining why the institution wants to keep the object private or secret. Have the students share their work with the class.

Have students re-read "Purpose of Lesson" on p. 64 of the text. Ask them to describe the extent to which they achieved the objectives of the lesson.

Using the Lesson

The activities suggested in "Using the Lesson" on p. 66 of the text reinforce or extend what students have learned about institutional privacy or secrecy. When working on any of the activities suggested, encourage students to analyze the following:

- what objects organizations and institutions might want to keep private or secret

- from whom they want to keep them private or secret

- how they keep the objects private or secret

- why they might want to keep the objects private or secret

You may have students work on these activities individually or in small groups. Have students share their work with the class.

This lesson concludes the study of Unit One, "What Is the Importance of Privacy?" If students are keeping a journal, have them write a summary in their journals of what they have learned about the importance of privacy to individuals and to institutions.

Optional Reinforcement and Enrichment Exercise

The scenario offered in the critical thinking exercise for this lesson, "The Nomination Committee," provides an excellent opportunity for students to practice conflict resolution skills. You may want students to try to resolve the dispute between the nominating committee and the principal using mediation. Three roles are involved:

- mediators
- Ricardo Ruiz, a member of the nominating committee
- Ms. Hunter, the principal of the school.

Directions for planning and conducting a mediation session can be found on p. 19 of this guide.

Unit Two: What Factors Explain Differences in Privacy Behavior?

Introduce Unit Two: What Factors Explain Differences in Privacy Behavior? Explain that this unit helps students understand that every individual in every culture seeks privacy. However, there are often great differences in the privacy behavior of individuals within a culture and among different cultures. First, students observe that people may choose to keep different **objects of privacy**, such as age, weight, or political and religious beliefs. Second, they observe that privacy behavior may differ with regard to the means people use to restrict access to objects of privacy, e.g., in one culture, custom may dictate ignoring others' private conversations held in public places, whereas in another culture such a custom might not exist.

Remind students that people differ in the objects they wish to keep private. They also differ in the ways they try to restrict access to these objects of privacy. Special circumstances in a person's life may explain this behavior.

Have students suggest from their experience some factors that might account for the differences in their own privacy behavior and that of others.

Have students read "Purpose of Unit" on p. 67 of the student text. Ask them to list three things they expect to learn from their study of Unit Two.

Lesson 4: Why Might People's Privacy Behavior Differ?

Lesson Overview

This lesson focuses on several factors that may be useful in explaining privacy behavior. Students learn the seven factors that typically influence a person's privacy behavior: family, occupation or role, individual experiences, opportunities for privacy, value placed on privacy, competing values, and individual differences. Students work in small groups to develop and apply their understanding of the factors that might cause people's privacy behavior to differ.

Lesson Objectives

At the conclusion of this lesson, students should be able to do the following:

- identify and explain factors that might influence privacy behavior
- describe similarities and differences in people's privacy behavior

Preparation/Materials Required

Student text pp. 68-70

Teaching Procedures

A. Introducing the Lesson

Introduce the lesson by directing attention to the illustrations on pp. 68-69 of the student text. Have students respond to the questions in the captions:

- How can family environment influence a person's privacy behavior?
- How can individual experiences influence a person's privacy behavior?

While you post the "Terms to Know" on the board, have students read "Purpose of Lesson" on p. 68 of the text.

B. Reading and Discussion

What factors influence privacy behavior?

Post on the board the seven factors, or elements, in people's lives that typically influence their privacy behavior:

- **family**
- **occupation** or **role**
- **individual experiences**
- **opportunities for privacy**
- **value placed on privacy**
- **competing values**
- **individual differences**

Have the class work in groups of three to five students. Assign each group one of the seven factors you wrote on the board. Ask the students to read about the factor and the examples that illustrate what it means on pp. 68-70 of the text, "What factors influence privacy behavior?" Ask students to identify the object of privacy and how the privacy is maintained in each situation they have read. Also ask students to think of examples to further illustrate each factor. Have each group share their responses with the class.

C. Critical Thinking Exercise

Examining Privacy Behavior

Have the students work with a study partner to answer the questions in the critical thinking exercise, "Examining Privacy Behavior," on p. 70 of the text. Read the directions for completing the exercise with the class. Encourage students to review the section, "What factors influence privacy behavior?" before answering the questions. Have the students share their responses with the class.

D. Concluding the Lesson

Have students re-read "Purpose of Lesson" on p. 68 of the text. Ask students to describe the extent to which they achieved the objectives of the lesson.

Using the Lesson

The activities suggested in "Using the Lesson" on p. 70 of the text reinforce or extend what students have learned about factors that influence people's privacy behavior.

All five activities suggested in this section can be completed by students individually or in small groups. Have students share their responses with the class.

Lesson 5: How Do Different Cultures Deal with Privacy?

Lesson Overview

Students identify and explain similarities and differences in privacy behavior between groups in two cultures. Students work in small groups to analyze a selection describing the privacy behavior of a group of people in Brazil. Then they describe the similarities and differences in privacy behavior between this group and their own culture. The concluding activity in the lesson focuses on the issue of privacy in George Orwell's novel, *1984*.

Lesson Objectives

At the conclusion of this lesson, students should be able to explain cultural similarities and differences in privacy behavior.

Preparation/Materials Required

Student text pp. 71-74

Optional: a copy for each student of "A Privacy Chart for the Mehinacu People" on p. 72 of the student text

---

Teaching Procedures

A. Introducing the Lesson

Introduce the lesson by directing attention to the photograph on p. 71 of the student text. Ask students to respond to the question in the caption, "How could you maintain a sense of privacy in a house with paper-thin walls?"

Remind students that although privacy behavior may differ among and within cultures, the need for privacy is found in all cultures.

While you post the "Term to Know" on the board, ask students to read "Purpose of Lesson" on p. 71 of the text.

B. Reading and Discussion
Differences Among Cultures

Have students read the section, "Differences Among Cultures," on p. 71 of the text. Ask students to define the term **culture**. Ask students to offer examples from the reading of different privacy behaviors in different cultures. Encourage students to offer examples from their experiences. If some cultural diversity exists in your classroom, you may want students from different cultures to share examples of privacy behavior practiced by people in their culture.

C. Critical Thinking Exercise
Examining Privacy Behavior

Have students work individually or with a study partner to complete the critical thinking exercise, "Examining Privacy Behavior," on p. 71 of the text. The reading selection, "The Mehinacu People," describes the privacy behavior of a group of people in Brazil.

Read the directions for completing the exercise with the class. Students may record their answers on a separate sheet of paper or you may make a copy for each student of "A Privacy Chart for the Mehinacu People" on p.72 in the student text. Possible answers to the questions in the exercise are included in the chart on page 78 in this guide. Have students share their answers with the class.

Conclude the discussion by asking the class to respond to the four questions in the "What do you think?" section on p. 73 of the text. Some responses that students might offer include the following:

1. What are some similarities and differences in the privacy behavior of the Mehinacu people compared with yours?

    ■ **Separation of the sexes at social occasions and religious ceremonies.** In our culture there are some social occasions that men or women may seek to restrict the opposite sex from attending. Most social functions, however, are mixed. Religious ceremonies are usually public and open to both men and women. Certain religious acts, such as confession or private prayer, require seclusion. Certain religious ceremonies such as orthodox Jewish services require the separation of women and men.

- **Living conditions.** We divide our homes into rooms that can be closed off from others, and individual family members often have private rooms. We enter others' homes only with the permission of the occupants.

- **Change in social status.** In our culture, this is usually a public event. Examples of change in social status events include election to office, weddings, confirmations, or Bar Mitzvahs.

2. What explanations can you give for these similarities and differences?

If students have difficulty with this question, ask what effect each of the following might have on the differences in privacy behavior between the two cultures:

- geography or climatic factors
- demographic factors such as population density
- economic factors such as needs and state of development
- technology
- social customs

3. Responses to question number 3 will vary depending on individual student experiences.

4. Responses to question number 4 will vary depending on individual student experiences.

D. Critical Thinking Exercise
Examining Privacy Behavior

The reading selection for the critical thinking exercise on pp. 73-74 of the text is a synopsis of George Orwell's novel *1984* that describes an imaginary society in which a Ruling Party controls human thought and action.

Direct attention to the illustration on p. 73 of the student text. Ask students to write a response in their journals to the question in the caption, "How would you feel if everything you did could be seen and heard?"

Have the class work in groups of three to four students to answer the questions in the "What do you think?" section of the exercise. Read the directions for completing the exercise with the class. Have students share their responses to the questions with the class. Some responses might include the following:

1. **What might people in this imaginary society want to keep private?**

Students should infer possible objects of privacy. Examples might include one's actions, conversations in the house, and the physical objects one might have in his or her home.

2. **How might they try to keep it private?**

Students should speculate about the various ways in which people might try to restrict access. Examples might include trying to get out of the field of vision of the telescreen, writing notes to each other instead of engaging in spoken conversations, and meeting in places where it would be less likely that they would be watched.

3. **What are some factors that might affect the privacy behavior of people in this imaginary society?**

Students should attempt to develop explanations and identify factors that might affect the privacy behavior of individuals in this society. Examples might include the following:

- the low value that the social and political culture seems to place on privacy
- the effect of technology
- the absence of political and legal institutions and processes designed to promote privacy, such as Fourth Amendment protections.

E. Concluding the Lesson

Have the students write a short story, not to exceed two handwritten pages. Ask them to imagine living in a highly technological society in the future. Ask them to create two objects they might want to keep private or secret. In their story they should briefly describe the objects of privacy and explain from whom and the way they would keep them private or secret. The story should describe the factors that affect the privacy behavior they have created. Have students share their stories with the class.

Have students re-read "Purpose of Lesson" on p. 71 of the text. Ask students to describe the extent to which they have achieved the objectives of the lesson.

A Privacy Chart for the Mehinacu People

What are the objects of privacy?	From whom are they to be kept private?	How are they to be kept private?
men's religious and social occasions	women of the group	ceremonies are held in a place from which women are restricted
individual homes	anyone who is not living in the home	a rule says that a person cannot go into any home that is not his or her own
certain areas within the house	certain family members	custom forbids certain family members from going into parts of the home
people who change social status	other group members	barriers are set up so that a person can be alone temporarily
misbehaviors—doing something wrong or illegal	other group members	custom requires that a person remain silent when someone is doing something wrong or illegal
bathing	other group members	there are designated bathing areas

Unit Three: What Are Some Benefits and Costs of Privacy?

Introduce **Unit Three: What Are Some Benefits and Costs of Privacy?** Explain that privacy carries with it certain benefits and costs for individuals, groups, and society. An understanding of the benefits and costs of privacy in general and in specific situations is essential in making intelligent decisions about the scope and limits of privacy.

Direct attention to the illustration on p. 75 of the student text. Ask students to respond to the question in the caption, "What might be some of the benefits and costs of a doctor or lawyer respecting the privacy of a client?"

Have students read "Purpose of Unit" on p. 75 of the text. Ask them to explain the importance of identifying the consequences of privacy in a given situation. Ask them to list two things they expect to learn from their study of Unit Three.

Lesson 6: What Are the Possible Consequences of Privacy?

Lesson Overview

Students learn to recognize the advantages and disadvantages of privacy in general and increase their ability to recognize the **benefits** and **costs** of privacy in specific situations. Examples of benefits of privacy that students learn include freedom, security, and protection of economic interests. Examples of costs of privacy that they learn include loneliness and alienation, financial costs, and opportunities for misbehavior and lawlessness. Students work in small groups to identify the consequences of privacy in particular situations and to label those consequences either as benefits or costs.

Lesson Objectives

At the conclusion of this lesson, students should be able to explain some common advantages and disadvantages of privacy.

Preparation/Materials Required

Student text pp. 76-80

Collect a series of news articles related to issues of privacy in your community, state, or the nation

Teaching Procedures

A. Introducing the Lesson

While you post the "Terms to Know" on the board, have students read "Purpose of Lesson" on p. 76 of the student text.

B. Critical Thinking Exercise
Identifying Consequences of Privacy

Have the class work in groups of three to five students. With the class, read the directions for completing the critical thinking exercise, "Identifying Consequences of Privacy," on p. 76 of the text. Have each group share its benefits and costs list with the class. Some responses might include the following:

1. The Fourth Amendment
   Benefits:
   - people might feel freer to do what they wanted in their homes
   - people might feel secure that their homes would not be invaded by officials without sufficient cause
   - people might develop an increased sense of individuality, autonomy, and/or personal dignity
   - guarantees of privacy might reduce the chances that a society would become authoritarian or **totalitarian**

   Costs:
   - guarantees of privacy might permit the planning and carrying out of criminal activities
   - the police might be hindered in their ability to enforce the law

2. School records
   Benefits:
   - students might feel secure that other students will not be allowed to look at their records
   - teachers or counselors who write in school records might feel greater freedom to express their thoughts in a more frank and open manner
   - if school records are a more honest appraisal of the students because they are kept private, then school personnel might be able to make better use of them in dealing with students

   Costs:
   - some students might resent the fact that there are records kept about them that they are not allowed to see
   - school records may contain inaccurate information that could be corrected if the records were made public

3. Lawyer confidentiality law
   Benefits:
   - clients might feel freer to discuss the facts of their case, which would enable the lawyer to represent them more effectively
   - clients might be able to trust their attorneys more completely

   Costs:
   - the proper authorities might be prevented from gaining access to valuable information about who is responsible for committing crimes

4. Carol's bereavement
   Benefits:
   - Carol might feel freer to express her feelings since she knows no one will overhear her
   - Carol might avoid embarrassment by not crying in front of others

   Costs:
   - Carol's friends cannot comfort her if she does not tell them what is wrong
   - Carol might feel lonely or alienated if she does not share her troubles with her friends
   - Carol's friends might feel resentment at being excluded or might feel "put out" by her unexplained moodiness

Explain that although people might agree on the benefits and costs of privacy in a certain situation, they might disagree on which benefits or costs are most important. For example, in the third situation, most people would agree that keeping information private might have the cost of preventing proper authorities from obtaining valuable information but have the benefit of allowing for an open relationship between lawyer and client essential to protect individual rights. However, some might think the benefit of obtaining information to apprehend criminals is more important than the cost of endangering the rights of an accused person.

C. Reading and Discussion
Examining Consequences of Privacy
Benefits of Privacy

Have students read "Examining Consequences of Privacy" and "Benefits of Privacy" on pp. 77-78 of the student text. Post the following benefits of privacy on the board:

- **freedom**
- **security**
- **protection of economic interests**
- **individuality**
- **creativity**
- **intimacy**

Ask the class to define each benefit listed and to offer examples from their reading or personal experience that illustrate each definition.

Direct attention to the five illustrations on pp. 77-78 of the text. Ask the class to respond to the questions in each of the captions:

- How might privacy protect freedom of belief and thought?
- How might privacy help people protect their plans and ideas?
- How can privacy remove the pressure to conform to others' views?
- How might privacy help people be creative?
- How can privacy help people develop close friendships?

D. Critical Thinking Exercise
Examining Benefits of Privacy

Have students work with a study partner to respond to the questions in the critical thinking exercise, "Examining Benefits of Privacy," on p. 78 of the text. Ask students to share their answers with the class.

E. Reading and Discussion
Costs of Privacy

Have students read "Costs of Privacy" on pp. 79-80 of the text. Post the following costs of privacy on the board:

- **loneliness and alienation**
- **loss of stimulation and intellectual growth**
- **misbehavior and lawlessness**
- **financial costs**
- **lack of accountability**

Ask the class to define each cost listed and to offer examples from their reading or personal experience that illustrate each definition.

Direct attention to the three illustrations on p. 79 of the text. Ask the class to respond to the questions in each of the captions:

- Do you think too much privacy can lead to loneliness?
- How might privacy interfere with intellectual growth?
- How might privacy create opportunities for crime?

F. Critical Thinking Exercise
Examining Costs of Privacy

Have students work with a study partner to respond to the questions in the critical thinking exercise, "Examining Costs of Privacy," on p. 80 of the text. Ask the students to share their answers with the class.

G. Concluding the Lesson

Give each student or pair of students a news article on an issue of privacy in your community, state, or the nation. Have students read the articles and identify the possible consequences of privacy. Ask them to label each consequence as a benefit or a cost. Have the students share their work with the class and then post their articles on your privacy bulletin board.

Have students re-read "Purpose of Lesson" on p. 76 of the text. Ask them to describe the extent to which they achieved the objectives of the lesson.

Using the Lesson

The activities suggested in "Using the Lesson" on p. 80 of the text reinforce or extend what students have learned about identifying the consequences of privacy and classifying those consequences as benefits or costs. Students can complete these activities individually or in small groups. Have students share their work with the class.

Optional Reinforcement and Enrichment Exercise

Refer students to the first situation on p. 76 of the text comparing **Writs of Assistance** and the Fourth Amendment. Post the following list of groups on the board:

- Civic Homeowners
- Rights of Citizens Union
- Police Department
- Citizens Against Crime Club

Assign students to one of the four groups. Ask each group to prepare a brief presentation on which benefits and costs are most and least important from the point of view of the organization they represent. Have each group select a spokesperson to present its opinion to the class. Conclude by reminding the class that they should consider various viewpoints in addition to their own when thinking about the benefits and costs of privacy.

Lesson 7: What Might Be Some of the Benefits and Costs of Confidentiality?

Lesson Overview

Students get additional practice in identifying consequences of privacy and classifying them as benefits or costs. The reading selection in the lesson describes a situation in which a middle-school student requests that his teacher keep confidential important information concerning who is responsible for a series of thefts in the school. During the critical thinking exercise, students identify the consequences of privacy in this situation and take and defend a position on what the student and the teacher might do to resolve the dilemma.

Lesson Objectives

At the conclusion of this lesson, students should be able to do the following:

- identify the consequences of privacy in a specific situation
- classify the consequences as benefits or costs
- take and defend a position on this issue of privacy

Preparation/Materials Required

Student text pp. 81-83

Teaching Procedures

A. Introducing the lesson

Ask students if they or someone they know ever encountered a situation in which someone shared important confidential information and had to decide whether or not to reveal the information. Have students share their experiences with the class, being cautious, of course, not to compromise anyone's right to privacy. Ask students how they decided what to do in those situations. Explain that the story they are about to read involves a similar dilemma.

Have students read "Purpose of Lesson" on p. 81 of the student text.

B. Reading and Discussion
Evaluating Benefits and Costs of Privacy

Have the class read "Evaluating Benefits and Costs of Privacy" on p. 81 of the text. Ask students to offer suggestions on how evaluating the benefits and costs of privacy can help us make decisions about issues of privacy.

Remind students that before we can make decisions about issues of privacy, we need to decide which consequences of privacy are most important to us. Remind them that people may disagree about which benefits and costs of protecting privacy in a particular situation are most important.

C. Critical Thinking Exercise
Crime and Confidentiality

Have the students work with a study partner to complete the critical thinking exercise, "Crime and Confidentiality," on p. 81 of the student text. The reading selection, "The School Locker Case," describes a situation in which a middle-school student shares information with his teacher concerning who is responsible for a series of thefts in the school. Since the student is fearful for his safety, he asks the teacher to keep the information confidential. Read the directions for completing the exercise with the class. Ask students to share with the class their responses to the questions in "Identifying Benefits and Costs" on p. 83 of the text. Some responses students might offer include the following:

1. List four or five possible consequences of Bernard and Mr. Pitts keeping their secret.
   Benefits:
   - Bernard will trust Mr. Pitts and feel freer to discuss this and other subjects with him that he wishes to keep secret
   - the thieves are less likely to injure Bernard if the information is kept secret

- Mr. Pitts will avoid loss of self-esteem that might occur if he revealed Bernard's secret and broke his commitment to him

Costs:

- the information about the thieves will not be available to authorities responsible for enforcing the law, such as the school principal and the police
- the thefts probably will continue
- Bernard and Mr. Pitts will not be living up to their responsibility to reveal the information to other students, school authorities, and the police
- Bernard and Mr. Pitts each may feel guilt, shame, or a loss of self-esteem as a result of feeling that he is not doing the right thing

2. Write a "B" next to each consequence you consider to be a benefit and a "C" next to each cost.

   Students will follow their own judgement in answering this question.

3. What do you think Mr. Pitts should do in this situation? What should Bernard do?

   Encourage students to support their responses with evidence from the story and with their benefit/cost analysis of the consequences of keeping the information regarding the school thefts secret.

D. Concluding the Lesson

To conclude the lesson, have students write an ending to "The School Locker Case" in which they take and defend a position on what the characters in the story should do to resolve the dilemma. Instruct them to include a discussion in their story of the consequences of privacy in this situation, identifying benefits and costs of each. If students are keeping journals, this assignment can be written there. Have student share their endings to the story with the class.

Have students re-read "Purpose of Lesson" on p. 81 of the text. Ask them to describe the extent to which they achieved the objectives of the lesson.

Using the Lesson

The activities suggested in "Using the Lesson" on p. 83 of the text reinforce or extend students' abilities to determine the consequences of privacy in a particular situation and to use the benefits and costs of those consequences to take and defend a position on an issue of privacy. Students can complete each activity individually or in small groups. Have students share their work with the class.

Lesson 8: What Might Be Some of the Benefits and Costs of the Government Keeping a Secret?

Lesson Overview

Students get additional practice in identifying the consequences of privacy and classifying them as benefits or costs. The reading selection in the critical thinking exercise describes a hypothetical dispute involving institutional privacy when the **Food and Drug Administration (FDA)** refuses to tell the public if it is conducting an investigation concerning the Drowsy Drug Company's sleeping tablets. Students role-play different points of view by taking and defending positions to determine whether the FDA should make the information public.

Lesson Objectives

At the conclusion of this lesson, students should be able to do the following:

- examine the benefits and costs of allowing an agency of the federal government to keep secrets
- explain the usefulness of considering benefits and costs in evaluating, taking, and defending positions on issues of privacy
- explain why people in different positions might value benefits and costs of privacy differently

Preparation/Materials Required

Student text pp. 84-86

Teaching Procedures

A. Introducing the lesson

Ask the class if they know or have heard of any situation in which an institution such as a corporation or government agency kept information secret from consumers or the general public. Ask students how they might decide what to do in such a situation. Explain that the story they are about to read involves a similar dilemma.

While you post the "Terms to Know" on the board, have the class read "Purpose of Lesson" on p. 84 of the student text.

B. Critical Thinking Exercise
Examining Governmental Privacy

This critical thinking exercise, "Examining Governmental Privacy," on pp. 84-85 of the student text involves role-playing a hearing before the Food and Drug Administration. The purpose of the hearing is to determine whether or not the agency should tell the public if it is conducting an investigation of a sleep-inducing drug available without prescription. The reading selection, "Dream-On Sleeping Tablets," describes the details of this imaginary dispute.

Have the class read "Examining Governmental Privacy" on pp. 84-85 of the student text. Ask students to recite the facts in the dispute, identifying the object of privacy, who wants to keep the information secret, and why they want to keep it secret. Ask students to describe how the government is maintaining privacy. Record their responses on the board. You may want to explain in greater detail the Food and Drug Administration's role in protecting the American people from potentially harmful or useless foods and drugs.

Ask the class to identify the consequences of maintaining secrecy in this situation. Record their responses on the board. Some of the responses students might offer include the following:

- Drowsy Drug Company would not lose customers and money
- people might continue taking the sleeping pills and continue getting headaches
- people would not be able to come forward with information that might be useful to the FDA in conducting the investigation
- the public would have no way to monitor the course of the investigation

- more generally, companies would not be tempted to interfere with competitors' businesses by instigating baseless FDA investigations of their competitors' products

Leave the list of consequences of privacy in this situation on the board for students to use during their preparation for the role-play.

Post the four roles on the board:

- Citizens for Safe Drugs
- The Drowsy Drug Company
- National Association of Drug Store Owners
- The Food and Drug Administration

Read the directions with the class for preparing and participating in the hearing, "Role-Playing Different Points of View," on pp. 85-86 of the student text. Check students' understanding of the instructions for preparing and participating in the activity. Divide the class into the four groups listed on the board. Allow adequate preparation time before commencing the hearing.

You will find a detailed description and instructions on role-playing an administrative hearing on p. 12 of this guide.

C. Concluding the Lesson

To conclude the lesson, ask students to determine whether or not the FDA should release the information requested by the public. Ask them to support their positions with evidence they heard during the role-play.

Have the class evaluate the presentations given by the groups by asking students to identify strong and weak arguments made on each side of the issue. Ask students to explain why different groups took different positions on the benefits and costs of privacy in this situation. Some responses might include the following:

- to protect economic interests
- to increase the availability of information regarding the product
- to increase the availability of information to the investigating team
- to increase the accountability of the agency and the company to consumers

Conclude by reminding the class of the importance of considering various viewpoints in addition to their own when thinking about the benefits and costs of privacy.

Have students re-read "Purpose of Lesson" on p. 84 of the text. Ask students to describe the extent to which they achieved the objectives of the lesson.

Using the Lesson

The activities suggested in "Using the Lesson" on p. 86 of the text reinforce or extend students' abilities to determine the consequences of privacy in a particular situation and to use the benefits and costs of those consequences to take and defend a position on the issue of privacy involved in that situation. Students can complete the activities individually or in small groups. Have the students share their work with the class.

This lesson concludes the study of Unit Three, "What Are Some Benefits and Costs of Privacy?" If students are keeping journals, have them write a summary in their journals of what they have learned about identifying the consequences of privacy and determining the benefits and costs of privacy in a particular situation. Also ask them to explain why it is important to consider different points of view when deciding issues of privacy.

Unit Four: What Should Be the Scope and Limits of Privacy?

Introduce **Unit Four: What Should Be the Scope and Limits of Privacy?** Explain that this unit will help students understand and apply a procedure useful in analyzing issues involving privacy, evaluating alternative courses of action, and making decisions about what the scope and limits of privacy should be in specific situations.

Students learn that conflicts sometimes develop between an individual or institution making a claim to privacy and another individual or institution asserting an interest or right to know with respect to the object of that claim of privacy. Students learn that in some cases it is reasonable and fair to deny privacy in favor of other values while in other cases privacy should be protected. To make an intelligent decision in any given situation involving a conflict about privacy, it is necessary to analyze the conflict and evaluate various ways of dealing with it before making decisions about how the conflict should be resolved. The procedures for analyzing a conflict about privacy and evaluating various ways of dealing with it are called "intellectual tools." For more details on the nature and purpose of intellectual tools, please see p. 6 of this guide.

Direct attention to the illustrations on p. 87 of the student text. Ask students to identify who is asserting a claim to privacy in each illustration. Ask students to identify who is asserting an interest or right to know with respect to each claim to privacy depicted in the illustrations.

Remind students that some of the most important issues we face as citizens involve questions about the scope and limits of privacy. These issues often arise between individuals or groups wishing to maintain privacy and others who claim the right to know something being kept private. In some cases, it is reasonable and fair to protect privacy. In other cases, other values and interests may be more important.

Have students read "Purpose of Unit" on p. 87 of the student text. Ask them to list two things they can expect to learn from their study of Unit Four.

Lesson 9: What Intellectual Tools Are Useful in Dealing with Issues of Privacy?

Lesson Overview

Students are introduced to a procedure useful in analyzing conflicts about privacy, evaluating alternative courses of action, and making decisions about what the scope and limits of privacy should be in specific situations. The steps involved in this procedure are called intellectual tools. The critical thinking exercise in the lesson introduces students to this procedure.

Lesson Objectives

At the conclusion of this lesson, students should be able to do the following:

- understand the purpose for using intellectual tools in examining a conflict about an issue of privacy
- use intellectual tools in evaluating, taking, and defending positions on issues of privacy

Preparation/Materials Required

Student text pp. 88-91

A copy for each student of the chart, "Intellectual Tools to Develop a Position on an Issue of Privacy," on p. 91 of this guide

---

Teaching Procedures

A. Introducing the Lesson

Ask the class to describe a conflict involving privacy in your school or community. Ask students to suggest the type of information they might need to analyze and resolve the conflict. Remind the class that during this lesson they will be learning a set of procedures to help them resolve a conflict of privacy.

While you post the "Terms to Know" on the board, have the class read "Purpose of Lesson" on p. 88 of the student text.

B. Reading and Discussion
When should government be able to invade the privacy of your home?

Have the class read "When should government be able to invade the privacy of your home?" on p. 88 of the student text. Ask students to identify some values and interests discussed in the reading that might conflict with the Fourth Amendment right to privacy inside our homes. Ask students why it might be important to decide when privacy should be supported or when it should give way to other values or interests. Help them understand the following:

- privacy can be instrumental in fostering other values such as freedom, intimacy, individuality, creativity, and trust
- privacy may conflict with other important values and interests, such as the right to know and the need to gain information to apprehend lawbreakers

Since we live in a constitutional democracy, citizens have the right to participate in making decisions regarding their right to privacy and the rights of others. Stress the importance of knowing enough about the subject to participate intelligently.

C. Critical Thinking Exercise
Identifying Conflicting Values and Interests

Have students work with a study partner to respond to the questions in the critical thinking exercise, "Identifying Conflicting Values and Interests," on p. 89 of the text. The selection, "John Barnes," describes how privacy is an important part of the life of a United States citizen named John Barnes. Barnes, however, is suspected of being the leader of a gang of criminals. With the class read the directions for completing the exercise. Have students share their responses to the questions in the "What do you think?" section of the exercise.

D. Reading and Discussion
Intellectual Tools: Things to Consider in Analyzing Issues of Privacy

Explain that the next few exercises help students become aware of the considerations and procedures useful in analyzing, evaluating, and making decisions regarding issues of privacy.

Post the four considerations often relevant to resolving conflicts about privacy on the board:

- **consent**
- **legality**
- **legal obligations**
- **moral obligations**

Explain that these considerations refer to some privacy conflicts where special circumstances may influence decisions about how the conflict should be resolved. For example, if the police have obtained lawfully a search **warrant** to search a particular house, then this special circumstance gives them a legal right to invade privacy in this limited way.

Introduce the concept of intellectual tools. An explanation of intellectual tools can be found on p. 5 of this guide. Have the class read "Intellectual Tools: Things to Consider in Analyzing Issues of Privacy" on pp. 89-90 of the text. Ask students to define and offer examples from the reading that illustrate the four considerations you posted on the board.

Direct attention to the three illustrations on pp. 89-90 of the text. Ask students to respond to the questions in the captions:

- How can consent justify an invasion of privacy?
- How can a search warrant justify an invasion of privacy?
- How can legal obligations require doctors to keep their patients' medical records private?

E. Critical Thinking Exercise
Examining Relevant Considerations

Have the class read the critical thinking exercise, "Examining Relevant Considerations," on p. 91 of the student text. The reading selection, "The Search," describes a United States Supreme Court case, *Chimel v. California*, concerning the search of Chimel's entire

house in connection with his arrest for burglary. Ask students to identify the facts in the case, such as the following:

- who wanted privacy in the case
- what they wanted to keep private
- how they tried to keep their privacy
- why they wanted privacy
- who wanted to invade the privacy
- how they invaded the privacy
- why they wanted to invade the privacy

Record their responses on the board. Leave this material on the board to use in the final critical thinking exercise of this lesson, "Using Intellectual Tools to Develop a Position," on p. 92 of the text.

Have the class work in groups of three to five students to answer the questions in the "What do you think?" section of the exercise. Have students share their responses with the class. Some responses might include the following:

1. **Did Mr. or Mrs. Chimel consent to the search of their house by the police?**

    Chimel's wife let the officers enter the house. Chimel objected when the officers asked permission to look around.

2. **Did the police have a legal right to search the Chimel's house?**

    There might be legal justification to search an arrestee's person and the immediate area where a weapon might be concealed. However, the police did not have a legal right to search the house since they did not have a search warrant.

3. **Did the police have a legal obligation not to search the Chimel's house?**

    The police had a legal obligation to comply with the Constitution, which required them to obtain a search warrant before they searched the Chimel's house.

4. **Did the police have a moral obligation not to search the Chimel's house?**

    The police could have searched Chimel and the areas immediately around him but not the rest of the house, thus ensuring their safety but not unnecessarily interfering with the Chimel's privacy.

F. Reading and Discussion
Intellectual Tools: A Procedure for Analyzing Issues of Privacy

Have the class read "Intellectual Tools: A Procedure for Analyzing Issues of Privacy" on p. 92 of the student text. While students complete their reading, post the five-step procedure for analyzing issues of privacy on the board.

1. **Identify the person claiming privacy.**

2. **Identify the persons wishing to invade the other's privacy.**

3. **Examine relevant considerations.**

4. **Evaluate alternative means of managing the issue.**

5. **Take and defend a position.**

Ask students to identify the information they are seeking in each of the five steps.

G. Critical Thinking Exercise
Using Intellectual Tools to Develop a Position

Have the class work in groups of three to five students to apply the five-step procedure for analyzing issues of privacy in *Chimel v. California*. Distribute to each student a copy of the chart, "Intellectual Tools to Develop a Position on an Issue of Privacy," on the next page of this guide. With the class read the directions for completing the exercise. Have students share their responses.

H. Concluding the Lesson

Direct attention to the illustration on p. 91 of the student text. Ask students to write a brief response to the question in the caption, "How can you evaluate a search of someone's home by police?"

Have students re-read "Purpose of Lesson" on p. 88 of the text. Ask them to describe the extent to which they achieved the objectives of the lesson.

Using the Lesson

The activities suggested in "Using the Lesson" on p. 93 of the student text reinforce or extend what students have learned about using intellectual tools to develop a position on an issue of privacy. The activities may be completed individually or in small groups.

Optional Reinforcement and Enrichment Exercises

You may invite a community resource person, such as a police officer, judge, or lawyer to the classroom to assist students with their analysis of *Chimel v. California.*

You also may want the class to role-play an appellate hearing in the case. Have the class divide into triads, groups of three. Assign one student to play the role of judge, another to present arguments for Chimel, and the third to present arguments for the state. Encourage students to use the intellectual tools to prepare their roles. After students present arguments for Chimel and for the state, call on the judge in each group to render a decision in the case. Have the judges share their decisions and reasoning with the class. For a detailed discussion on how to conduct a *pro se* court, refer to p. 16 of this guide.

Teacher References

Chimel v. California, 395 U.S. 752 (1969). During an arrest, can a warrantless search of an entire house be justified under the Fourth Amendment? By a 7-2 vote the Supreme Court said no. Justice Stewart wrote the majority opinion in the case. Such a search is unreasonable and contrary to the Fourth Amendment. An arresting officer may search the suspect to remove any weapons the arrestee might be carrying or to seize any evidence to prevent its destruction. A lawful search would include the immediate area from which the arrestee might gain access to a weapon or be able to conceal or destroy evidence.

Intellectual Tools to Develop a Position on an Issue of Privacy

1. Identify the person claiming privacy: Whose claim to privacy was endangered in this case? What objects did the person want to keep private? How might the person have kept the objects private? Why might the person want to keep the objects private?	
2. Identify the persons wishing to invade the other's privacy: Who wished to limit or invade the other's privacy? How did that person invade the other's privacy? Why did that person want to invade the other's privacy?	
3. Examine relevant considerations: Did the person consent to have his or her privacy invaded? Explain. Did the person who invaded the other's privacy have a legal right to do so? Why or why not? Did the person who invaded the other's privacy have a legal obligation not to do so? Why or why not? Did the person who invaded the other's privacy have a moral obligation not to do so? Why or why not?	
4. Evaluate alternative means of managing the issue: What are the costs and benefits of recognizing the person's claim to privacy? What are the costs and benefits of rejecting the claim to privacy? What are some other means the person who wants to invade the privacy might use to gather the information he or she needs? What are the benefits of each of these means? What are the costs of each of these means?	
5. Take and defend a position: What position would you take on the privacy issues in this case? Explain your reasoning.	

Lesson 10: What Conflicts About Privacy May Arise from Law Enforcement?

Lesson Overview

Students apply the considerations and procedures useful for resolving conflicts about privacy to a specific situation. The reading selection in the lesson describes a conflict arising from a state agency proposal to expand a hidden camera installation program in state forests to aid forest fire prevention. The activity of the lesson provides students with additional practice in using intellectual tools to develop a position on an issue of privacy.

Lesson Objectives

At the conclusion of this lesson, students should be able to use the intellectual tools to take and defend a position on an issue of privacy.

Preparation/Materials Required

Student text pp. 94-96

Optional: A copy for each student of the chart, "Intellectual Tools to Develop a Position on an Issue of Privacy," on p. 91 of this guide

Teaching Procedures

A. Introducing the Lesson

Direct attention to the illustration on p. 96 of the student text. Ask students to respond to the question in the caption, "What arguments can you make for and against the use of cameras to monitor students' behavior at school?" Explain that during this lesson the class will examine a similar situation in which a government agency wants to use hidden cameras to monitor people's behavior.

While you post the "Term to Know" on the board, have students read "Purpose of Lesson" on p. 94 of the student text.

B. Critical Thinking Exercise

Have the class work in groups of three to five students to complete the critical thinking exercise on pp. 94-95 of the text. Read the directions for completing the exercise with the class. The reading selection, "The Eye in the Forest," describes a conflict that surfaces when the California Division of Forestry proposes to expand a program for installing hidden cameras in the forest to aid in the apprehension of **arsonists**. Backpackers, hikers, and bird-watchers are concerned that the cameras will invade their privacy.

C. Reading and Discussion
Using Intellectual Tools to Develop a Position

Before students begin to work on the critical thinking exercise, review the five-step procedure, "Using Intellectual Tools to Develop a Position," on p. 95 of the text with the class. You might ask students to respond to the questions on a separate sheet of paper or give each student a copy of the "Intellectual Tools to Develop a Position on an Issue of Privacy" on p. 91 of this guide.

D. Concluding the Lesson

Ask students to share with the class their responses to the questions in the five-step procedure, "Using Intellectual Tools to Develop a Position."

Have student re-read "Purpose of Lesson" on p. 94 of the text. Ask them to describe the extent to which they achieved the objectives of the lesson.

Using the Lesson

The activities suggested in "Using the Lesson" on pp. 95-96 of the student text reinforce or extend what students have learned about using intellectual tools to evaluate different positions and to take and defend a position on an issue of privacy. During each activity, encourage students to use the five-step procedure for evaluating different positions and for taking and defending a position on an issue of privacy. All four activities suggest situations in which an institution, such as a government, a business, or a school, uses surveillance cameras to monitor people's actions. Students may complete these exercises individually or in small groups. Have students share their work with the class.

Lesson 11: What Conflicts About Privacy May Arise from Attempts by Government to Label People?

Lesson Overview

This lesson extends students' abilities to analyze conflicts about privacy, to evaluate alternative courses of action, and to make decisions about the scope and limits of privacy in a given situation. Students role-play a legislative debate on a proposed law requiring people convicted of certain crimes to wear a badge informing others of the crime they have committed.

Lesson Objectives

At the conclusion of this lesson, students should be able to do the following:

- evaluate different positions on an issue of privacy
- take and defend a position on an issue of privacy

Preparation/Materials Required

Student text pp. 97-100

Teaching Procedures

A. Introducing the Lesson

Direct attention to the illustrations on p. 97 of the student text. Ask students to describe how they might feel if they were required by law to wear such a label. Explain that this lesson involves a similar situation.

While you post the "Terms to Know" on the board, have students read "Purpose of Lesson" on p. 97 of the text.

B. Reading and Discussion
Labels and Privacy

Have the class read "Labels and Privacy" on pp. 97-98 of the text. Ask students why they think making a person wear a religious symbol might interfere with his or her privacy. Ask them to offer other examples from the reading or from personal experience where requiring people to wear labels interfered with their privacy. Ask students to think about reasons people convicted of crimes deserve to have their privacy rights protected. Ask whether labeling criminals is a fair and reasonable way for society to punish and to protect itself from those who disobey the law.

C. Critical Thinking Exercise
Labeling Convicted Criminals

Have students work with a study partner to complete the critical thinking exercise, "Labeling Convicted Criminals," on pp. 98-99 of the student text. The reading selection describes a **bill** the state legislature is considering that requires all persons convicted of a **felony** to wear a badge identifying their crime. With the class, read the directions for completing the exercise. Explain that this work is in preparation for role-playing a legislative debate.

D. Reading and Discussion
Using Intellectual Tools to Develop a Position

Before students begin to work on the critical thinking exercise, review with the class the five-step procedure, "Using Intellectual Tools to Develop a Position," on p. 99 of the text. You may have the students respond to the questions on a separate sheet of paper or give each student a copy of the chart, "Intellectual Tools to Develop a Position on an Issue of Privacy," on p. 91 of this guide. Ask students to share their responses.

E. Critical Thinking Exercise
Role-Playing a Legislative Debate

Post the three roles represented in the legislative debate on the board:

- urban legislators
- suburban legislators
- rural legislators

Have the class read "Role-Playing a Legislative Debate" on pp. 99-100 of the text. Review with the class the three roles and the instructions for participating in the legislative debate. Divide the class into groups representing the three roles. Allow adequate time for the groups to discuss the issues and for individual legislators to prepare their positions on whether or not to support the proposed bill. Some students may want to prepare **amendments** to the bill to introduce during the debate. In preparing their roles encourage students to use the information they gathered while working on the five-step procedure, intellectual tools.

You will find a detailed description and instructions for role-playing a legislative debate on p. 14 of this guide.

F. Concluding the Lesson

At the conclusion of the debate, take a vote of the class asking whether the students support or oppose the bill as amended. Ask students to explain why they have taken different positions on this issue of privacy. You may want students to write a brief explanation in their journals of their positions on this issue of privacy.

Have students re-read "Purpose of Lesson" on p. 97 of the text. Ask them to describe the extent to which they achieved the objectives of the lesson.

Using the Lesson

The activities suggested in "Using the Lesson" on p. 100 of the student text reinforce or extend what students have learned about using intellectual tools to evaluate different positions and to take and defend a position on an issue of privacy. The activities may be completed individually or in small groups. During each activity, encourage students to use the five-step procedure for evaluating different positions and for taking and defending a position on an issue of privacy. All three activities suggested in this section of the lesson describe situations in which an institution such as the government or the school requires people to accept some type of label.

Optional Reinforcement and Enrichment Exercise

You may invite a community resource person such as a state legislator or a lawyer to the classroom to assist students during their preparation for the legislative debate.

Lesson 12: What Privacy Rights Should Groups and Associations Have?

Lesson Overview

This lesson extends students' abilities to analyze conflicts about privacy, to evaluate alternative courses of action, and to make decisions about the scope and limits of privacy in a given situation. Students role-play a United States Supreme Court hearing in a case involving an organization that restricts its membership on the basis of **gender**, contrary to state law. The organization claims, as a private charitable group, that the law violates a right to **freedom of association**.

Lesson Objectives

At the conclusion of this lesson, students should be able to do the following:

- evaluate different positions on an issue of group privacy

- take and defend a position on an issue of group privacy

Preparation/Materials Required

Student text pp. 101-104

Teaching Procedures

A. Introducing the Lesson

Ask students if they are members of any school or community organizations. Ask them to explain how membership is determined and if anyone is prohibited from joining the group. Ask if the organization maintains any objects of privacy or secrecy. How might they feel if membership in the organization were regulated by law? Explain that in this lesson the class will examine a situation in which an organization restricted membership on the basis of gender, contrary to state law.

While you post the "Terms to Know" on the board, have students read "Purpose of Lesson" on p. 101 of the text.

B. Reading and Discussion
Conflicts About Privacy Rights of Groups

Have the class read "Conflicts About Privacy Rights of Groups" on p. 101 of the student text. Ask students to respond to the three questions in the introductory paragraph:

- How much privacy should a group or association have?

- Should a group be allowed to keep the identity of its members a secret?

- Should a group be able to decide for itself who may be a member?

Encourage students to offer examples from the reading and their experience.

Direct attention to the illustration on p. 102 of the student text. Ask students to respond to the question in the caption, "Why might the government require a group to admit women as members?"

C. Critical Thinking Exercise
Examining Group Privacy

Have the class read the critical thinking exercise, "Examining Group Privacy," on pp. 101-102 of the student text. The reading selection, "The United States Jaycees," describes a United States Supreme Court case, *Roberts v. United States Jaycees*, concerning a Minnesota law prohibiting discrimination against people on the basis of gender. The state said the law applied to the Jaycees, an all-male club, and required them to admit women as members. The Jaycees sued, claiming that they were a private charitable organization and the state had no right to interfere with their membership decisions. With the class read the directions for completing the exercise. Explain that this work is preparation for role-playing a United States Supreme Court hearing.

D. Reading and Discussion
Using Intellectual Tools to Develop a Position

Have the class work in groups of three to five students to complete the critical thinking exercise, "Examining

Group Privacy." Before students begin work on the exercise, review the five-step procedure, "Using Intellectual Tools to Develop a Position," on pp. 102-103 of the text. You may have the students respond to the questions on a separate sheet of paper or give each student a copy of the chart, "Intellectual Tools to Develop a Position on an Issue of Privacy," on p. 91 of this guide. Ask students to share their responses with the class.

E. Critical Thinking Exercise
Role-Playing a Supreme Court Hearing

Post the five roles represented in the mock Supreme Court hearing on the board:

- United States Supreme Court Justices
- Minnesota Attorney General's Office
- United States Jaycees
- National Association of Women Executives
- Association of American Golf and Tennis Clubs

Have the class read "Role-Playing a Supreme Court Hearing" on pp. 103-104 of the text. With the class review the five roles and the instructions for participating in the Supreme Court hearing. For more details on conducting a moot court, refer to p. 17 of this guide.

Divide the class into groups representing the five roles. Allow adequate time for the groups to discuss and prepare their positions on the issue. During the preparation period, the students representing the Justices should prepare questions to ask the other groups during the hearing. In preparing their roles encourage students to use the information they gathered while working on the five-step procedure, intellectual tools.

You may explain to the class that normally only the parties directly involved in a case such as the Minnesota Attorney General's Office and the United States Jaycees would present arguments before the Supreme Court. Other interested parties such as the National Association of Women Executives and the American Golf and Tennis Clubs might file *amicus*, or friends of the Court, briefs stating their positions on the issues. Having both the parties and the *amicus* briefs represented in this simulation is a pedagogical device to involve all students in the lesson.

F. Concluding the Lesson

After the students who role-played Supreme Court justices in *Roberts v. United States Jaycees* have deliberated the issues argued during the presentations, ask them to share their decision with the class. Ask them to explain the reasoning which supported the decision. Ask the class to evaluate the presentations by identifying strengths and weaknesses in the arguments made by the parties in the case. Ask students to explain the usefulness of using the five-step procedure, "Using Intellectual Tools to Develop a Position," in evaluating the issue of privacy in this situation and in taking and defending a position on the issue.

Have students re-read "Purpose of Lesson" on p. 101 of the text. Ask them to describe the extent to which they achieved the objectives of the lesson.

Using the Lesson

The activities suggested in "Using the Lesson" on p. 104 of the student text reinforce or extend what students have learned about using intellectual tools to evaluate different positions and to take and defend a position on an issue of privacy. The activities may be completed individually or in small groups. During each activity, encourage students to use the five-step procedure for evaluating different positions and for taking and defending a position on an issue of privacy. The two activities suggested in this section of the lesson describe situations in which an organization or institution might want to restrict or keep their membership secret.

Optional Reinforcement and Enrichment Exercises

You may invite a community resource person such as a judge or lawyer to the classroom to assist the students in preparing their arguments for role-playing a Supreme Court hearing. The community resource person also might join the panel of justices during oral presentations and assist with the class discussion following the activity.

Teacher References

Roberts v. United States Jaycees, 468 U.S. 609 (1984), Minnesota's Human Rights Act, which prohibits discrimination in places of public accommodation on the basis of gender, required the Jaycees to admit women as members. The Jaycees claimed that the law violated their constitutional right to freedom of association. The Supreme Court identified two types of freedom of association the Constitution protects: freedom of "intimate association" and freedom of "expressive association." The Constitution protects intimate associations because they are a fundamental element of personal liberty: they create the sort of personal bonds that are crucial in allowing people to define their own identities, and act as a buffer between the individual and the power of the state. Groups may or may not deserve protection as "intimate associations" depending on size, purpose, policies, selectivity, congeniality, and other factors.

Alternatively, if a group engages in protected First Amendment activities such as political speech, it will deserve protection as an "expressive association." Governmental interference with the internal organization or affairs of such groups are allowed only if necessary to achieve a compelling governmental interest, unrelated to the suppression of ideas.

Applying these principles, the Court ruled against the Jaycees. The Jaycees' organization was too large and unselective to justify protection as an "intimate association." While the Minnesota Human Rights Act clearly interfered with the Jaycees' internal structure and affairs, the law served the compelling government interest of eradicating gender discrimination.

Lesson 13: How Do Advances in Technology Threaten Privacy?

Lesson Overview

This lesson extends students' abilities to analyze conflicts about privacy, to evaluate alternative courses of action, and to make decisions about the scope and limits of privacy in a given situation. Students role-play a congressional hearing to receive recommendations on whether or not Congress should create a central government computer **data bank** combining the information all government agencies now have about every person in the country.

Lesson Objectives

At the conclusion of this lesson, students should be able to do the following:

- evaluate different positions on an issue of privacy involving technology
- take and defend a position on an issue of privacy involving technology

Preparation/Materials Required

Student text pp. 105-108

Teaching Procedures

A. Introducing the Lesson

Have the class think of situations in which technology has had an impact on their ability to keep something private or secret. Ask the students to share their experiences with the class. Ask students how they might feel if all information about them were kept in one central data bank accessible to anyone with a computer. Explain that in this lesson students will examine an imaginary proposal to create a central government data bank.

While you post the "Terms to Know" on the board, have students read "Purpose of Lesson" on p. 105 of the text.

B. Reading and Discussion
How do computers affect privacy?

Have the class read "How do computers affect privacy?" on pp. 105-106 of the student text. Direct attention to the photograph on p. 107 of the text. Ask students to respond to the question in the caption, "How do computers affect everyone's privacy?" Encourage students to offer examples from the reading and from their experience.

C. Critical Thinking Exercise
The Central Government Data Bank Proposal

Have the class read the critical thinking exercise, "The Central Government Data Bank Proposal," on pp. 106-107 of the student text. The reading selection describes a proposal to combine into one central government data bank information about every person in the country now contained in the separate computers of all government agencies. Thus, the information known to one agency would be available to all agencies throughout the United States. The selection explains some of the benefits and costs of creating a central government data bank. With the class read the directions for completing the exercise. Explain that this work is preparation for role-playing a congressional hearing on this issue of privacy.

D. Reading and Discussion
Using Intellectual Tools to Develop a Position

Have the students work with a study partner to complete the critical thinking exercise, "The Central Government Data Bank Proposal." Before students begin work on the exercise, review with the class the five-step procedure, "Using Intellectual Tools to Develop a Position," on p. 107 of the text. You may have students respond to the questions on a separate sheet of paper or give each student a copy of the "Intellectual Tools to Develop a Position on an Issue of Privacy" on p. 91 of this guide.

Ask students to share their responses with the class.

E. Critical Thinking Exercise
Role-Playing a Public Hearing

Post the five roles represented in the mock congressional hearing on the board:

- American Association of Computer Manufacturers
- Citizens for Greater Efficiency Committee
- Citizens for Privacy Committee
- People United Against Technology
- House Committee on Government Use of Data

Have the class read "Role-Playing a Public Hearing" on p. 108 of the text. Review the five roles and the instructions for participating in the congressional hearing with the class. Divide the class into groups representing the five roles. Allow adequate time for the groups to discuss and prepare their positions on the issue. In preparing their roles encourage students to use the information they gathered while working on the five-step procedure, intellectual tools.

You will find a detailed description and instructions on role-playing a congressional hearing on p. 12 of this guide.

F. Concluding the Lesson

At the conclusion of the congressional hearing take a vote of the class on whether they support or oppose the proposal to create a central government data bank. Ask students to explain why they have taken differing positions on this issue of privacy. You may want to have students explain briefly in their journals their positions on this issue of privacy.

Have student re-read "Purpose of Lesson" on p. 105 of the text. Ask them to describe the extent to which they achieved the objectives of the lesson.

Using the Lesson

The activities suggested in "Using the Lesson" on p. 108 of the student text reinforce or extend what students have learned about using intellectual tools to evaluate different positions and to take and defend a position on an issue of privacy. The activities may be completed individually or in small groups. Encourage students to use the five-step procedure for evaluating different positions and for taking and defending a position on an issue of privacy.

Optional Reinforcement and Enrichment Exercises

You may invite a community resource person such as a person in a position of authority within a government agency or a state legislator to the classroom to assist students in preparing their arguments for role-playing a congressional hearing. You might ask the community resource person to join the group role-playing the House Committee on Government Use of Data during the presentations and to assist with the class discussion following the activity.

Lesson 14:   How Useful Are Written Policies in Dealing with Issues of Privacy?

Teaching Procedures

A. Introducing the Lesson

While you post the "Terms to Know" on the board, have students read "Purpose of Lesson" on p. 109 of the text.

If you have not already done so, discuss the guidelines for learning about and discussing controversial issues with the class. You will find a set of guidelines for teaching controversial issues on p. 6 of this guide.

B. Reading and Discussion
Privacy and AIDS

Have the class read "Privacy and AIDS" on p. 109 of the student text. Direct attention to the photographs on pp. 109 and 110 of the text. Ask students to respond to the questions in the captions:

- How would you deal with the privacy needs of students like Ryan?
- Why might people with AIDS want to keep their medical condition private?

In response to this question, ask students to compare the reactions of people in the three communities discussed in the reading (Kokomo, Indiana; Swansea, Massachusetts; and Arcadia, Florida) to having students with AIDS attend classes in the public schools.

C. Critical Thinking Exercise
AIDS in the School

Have the class read the critical thinking exercise, "AIDS in the School," on pp. 110-111 of the student text. The reading selection describes the concerns of a fourteen-year-old boy, Nathan, when he learns that he is HIV-positive. Nathan and his parents meet with the superintendent of schools to request that Nathan's medical condition be kept strictly confidential. Mr. Brown, the superintendent, considers the issues he might face when Nathan enrolls in school that fall. Read the directions with the class for completing the exercise. Explain that this work is in preparation for an activity in which the class will create a school policy to deal with the situation.

D. Reading and Discussion
Using Intellectual Tools to Develop a Position

Have the students work with a study partner to complete the critical thinking exercise, "AIDS in the School." Before students begin work on the exercise, review with the class the five-step procedure, "Using Intellectual Tools to Develop a Position," on pp. 111-112 of the text. You may have students respond to the questions on a separate sheet of paper or give each student a copy of the "Intellectual Tools to Develop a Position on an Issue of Privacy" on p. 91 of this guide.

E. Reading and Discussion
Using Policies to Resolve Conflicts

Explain that institutions frequently establish a policy—guidelines, rules, directions—to deal with an issue that comes up repeatedly. Direct attention to the illustration on p. 112 of the student text. Ask students to respond to the question in the caption, "How can dress codes and other policies help institutions be consistent in dealing with problems?" Have the class read "Using Policies to Resolve Conflicts" on p. 112 of the text. Ask students to offer examples from the reading or from their experience with institutions that establish policies, as well as examples of some of those policies. Ask students what they think might be some benefits and costs of having a policy to deal with an issue that comes up again and again.

F. Critical Thinking Exercise
Establishing a School Policy on Privacy

On the board post the six categories of people who need to be considered in establishing a school policy on AIDS:

- school administrators
- the student's teachers and guidance counselor
- other teachers and guidance counselors
- other school employees
- students
- parents

Have the class read the critical thinking exercise, "Establishing a School Policy on Privacy," on pp. 112-113 of the student text.

With the class review the three issues that the policy should address:

- Who should be told that a student has enrolled who has AIDS or who is HIV-positive?
- Who should be told the student's name?
- What should be done to make sure that people who are told the student's name do not repeat the information to others?

Divide the class into groups of five students and ask them to respond to the questions. Emphasize that each group is to consider the privacy needs of HIV-positive students as well as the needs of others for information. Allow adequate time for the groups to discuss and prepare their positions. Ask the groups to share their responses with the class. Record their responses on the board. You may want the groups to record their responses on chart paper and then report their responses to the class.

Distribute to each student a copy of the "Middle School/Junior High School Policy on Students Infected with HIV" chart on p. 114 of the student text. Lead a class discussion on each of the issues listed. Encourage students to defend positions they might take on a given issue with the reasoning that supports that position. It may be necessary to remind students, from time to time, what it means to achieve group **consensus** on an issue. After the class reaches consensus on an issue, have the students record the information on their charts.

G. Concluding the Lesson

After the class has completed its work, have the students evaluate the policy they created. Ask the students to review their charts and respond to the following questions:

- Does the policy provide information that a student who is HIV-positive has enrolled in the school to those people who have a need to know?

- Does the policy reveal the information and the student's name only to those people who have a need to know?

- Does the policy make sure that the privacy rights of students who are HIV-positive are adequately protected?

- Does the policy establish appropriate guidelines or rules for resolving this issue now and in the future?

- Does the policy resolve this conflict about privacy in a manner that is fair to all parties concerned?

You may also want students to evaluate the process they have experienced in creating a policy for the school. Ask students to respond to the following questions:

- What might be some of the benefits of participating in making policy decisions for the school?

- What might be some of the disadvantages of participating in making policy decisions?

- What might be done in the future to maximize the benefits but minimize the disadvantages?

- Why might it be important for citizens to develop policy-making skills?

Have student re-read "Purpose of Lesson" on p. 109 of the text. Ask them to describe the extent to which they achieved the objectives of the lesson.

Using the Lesson

The activities suggested in "Using the Lesson" on p. 113 of the student text reinforce or extend what students have learned about establishing a policy to deal with issues that might arise repeatedly. The activities may be completed individually or in small groups.

This lesson concludes the study of Unit Four, "What Should Be the Scope and Limits of Privacy?" Have students write a summary in their journals of what they have learned about when it is reasonable and fair to protect privacy and when privacy may have to yield to other more important values and interests. Also have them evaluate the usefulness of applying intellectual tools to analyzing, taking, and defending a position on an issue of privacy.

Optional Reinforcement and Enrichment Exercises

You may want the class to present the policy they developed to the principal or other interested persons in the school or administration. Allow time for the class to organize, prepare, and practice their presentation.

Concluding the Privacy Curriculum

This concludes the study of the Privacy curriculum. It will be valuable to both you and your students to reflect on and evaluate the total experience with this section of *Foundations of Democracy*, including the content and the instruction methods. Distribute a copy to each student of "Reflecting on Your Experience" on p. 28 of this guide. Remind students that they should not only reflect on and evaluate their experiences, but also those of the class. Have students share their responses with the class.

The Responsibility Curriculum

Introduce the Responsibility curriculum. This curriculum presents an overview of responsibility as a concept intrinsic not only to a democratic society but also to society itself. If individuals fail to exercise or assume personal responsibility, and if nothing exists to take their place, then society as an entity no longer exists; it is merely a collection of separate unbridled individuals. On the other hand, if responsibility for personal actions is taken away from the private individual and turned over to others, it is a tacit admission that ordinary individuals cannot or should not control their destiny. Therefore, they are not free.

Against such a background, this curriculum provides students with an increased awareness of the importance of responsibility in their lives and its place in contemporary society, and encourages their capacity and inclination to deal effectively and wisely with issues of responsibility.

Direct attention to the photograph on p. 116 of the student text. Ask students to create a list of responsibilities President Clinton acquired when he became the nation's forty-second president. List their responses on the board. Ask students to explain where they think these responsibilities come from.

Have the class read "Introduction" on p. 116 of the text. Discuss the responsibilities President Clinton called on each citizen to fulfill in his inaugural address. Where do these responsibilities come from? How can citizens decide which responsibilities to fulfill?

Unit One: What Is the Importance of Responsibility?

Introduce Unit One: What Is the Importance of Responsibility? The purpose of this unit is to help students understand the importance of responsibility to society and to the individual. Students learn the numerous sources of responsibility and the various ways we express responsibility in our society.

Direct attention to the illustration on p. 117 of the student text. Ask students to respond to the question in the caption, "Why is it important to fulfill responsibilities?" Conclude the discussion by asking students to offer reasons it might be important to study responsibility.

Have the class read "Purpose of Unit" on p. 117 of the text. Ask students to list three things they expect to learn from their study of Unit One. If students are keeping a journal they can record their list in their journals. Review these journal notations at the conclusion of the study of responsibility. Repeat this activity during the introductions to Units Two, Three, and Four.

Lesson 1: What Is Responsibility?

Lesson Overview

Students are introduced to the concept of **responsibility** and its importance in daily life. Students learn that responsibility includes a duty or obligation to do something or not to do something. They learn that different consequences might result from fulfilling and not fulfilling responsibilities. During the critical thinking exercise students read and discuss situations that raise issues of responsibility. Analysis of those situations includes identifying the following:

- the responsibilities
- to whom they are owed
- their **sources**
- the rewards or penalties that might be associated with fulfilling or not fulfilling them

Lesson Objectives

At the conclusion of this lesson, students should be able to do the following:

- define the term **responsibility**
- identify examples of responsibilities
- identify and describe possible sources of these responsibilities
- identify and describe rewards commonly related to fulfillment of these responsibilities
- identify and describe penalties related to failure to fulfill these responsibilities

Preparation/Materials Required

Student text pp. 118-119

Teaching Procedures

A. Introducing the Lesson

Ask students to list five of the most common responsibilities they have. Then have them identify the following:

- the **reward** they might receive for fulfilling the responsibilities
- the **penalties** they might receive for failing to fulfill those responsibilities
- the sources of each of the responsibilities

Ask students to explain the possible consequences to others of fulfilling or not fulfilling their responsibilities.

Ask students to list five responsibilities other people have towards them. Ask students to describe what might be the consequences to themselves if these responsibilities are not fulfilled.

While you post the "Terms to Know" on the board, have the class read "Purpose of Lesson" on p. 118 of the student text.

B. Reading and Discussion
What is responsibility?

Have the class read "What is responsibility?" on p. 118 of the text. Help students understand the definition of responsibility as it is used in this curriculum. Ask students to cite examples from their experience of a duty or obligation to do something. Also ask them to cite examples of a duty or obligation not to do something. Ask them to identify some of the **rewards** or benefits that come from fulfilling responsibilities. Ask them to identify a **penalty** or punishment that may be imposed for failure to fulfill a responsibility.

C. Critical Thinking Exercise
Examining Responsibilities

Have students work individually or with a study partner to complete the critical thinking exercise,

"Examining Responsibilities," on pp. 118-119 of the text. With the class read the directions for completing the exercise and review the questions in the "What do you think?" section on p. 119. After students have completed the exercise, ask them to share their responses with the class. Record their responses on the board.

D. Reading and Discussion
Why is responsibility important?

Have the class read "Why is responsibility important?" on p. 119 of the text. With the class review the questions in the "What do you think?" section on p. 119. You may allot class time for students to develop responses to the questions or assign the exercise as homework. Have students share their work with the class.

E. Concluding the Lesson

To conclude the lesson, encourage students to speculate on the character of a world without responsibility. What might life be like at home, at school, and in the community if no one accepted or fulfilled responsibilities to other people?

Have the class re-read "Purpose of Lesson" on p. 118 of the text. Ask students to describe the extent to which they achieved the objectives of the lesson.

Using the Lesson

The activities suggested in "Using the Lesson" on p. 119 of the text reinforce or extend what students have learned about the following:

- identifying responsibilities
- determining to whom they are owed
- identifying the sources of those responsibilities
- identifying consequences of fulfilling or not fulfilling them

You may have students complete these exercises individually or in small groups. Ask students to share their work with the class.

Lesson 2: What Are Some Sources of Responsibility?

Lesson Overview

Students learn that responsibilities come from a number of common sources, such as promises, **assignments, occupation,** and law. Students also learn how and why people assume specific responsibilities. During the critical thinking exercise, students identify responsibilities from their experience. For each responsibility identified, they determine if the responsibility was chosen voluntarily, was imposed, or was assumed without conscious or deliberate thought.

Lesson Objectives

At the conclusion of this lesson, students should be able to do the following:

- identify and describe different sources of responsibility
- explain how people assume specific responsibilities

Preparation/Materials Required

Student text pp. 120-123

Teaching Procedures

A. Introducing the Lesson

Direct attention to the illustrations on pp. 120-122 of the text. Ask students to identify the responsibilities shown in the illustrations. Ask students to identify the responsibility, to whom it is owed, and the possible source of that responsibility.

While you post the "Terms to Know" on the board, have students read "Purpose of Lesson" on p. 120 of the text.

B. Reading and Discussion
Sources of Responsibility

Have the class read "Sources of Responsibility" on pp. 120-122 of the text. Post the following terms on the board:

1. promises
2. assignments
3. appointment
4. occupation
5. law
6. custom
7. citizenship
8. moral principles

Ask students to explain each of these common sources of responsibility and to offer examples from their reading that illustrate each source. Help students understand that promises create an **obligation** to keep the promise, that promises may take the form of **contracts** or legal agreements, and that when people make a promise they **consent** to fulfill the obligation.

Discuss with the class how people assume responsibilities. Help students understand that people might assume responsibilities voluntarily (promises). Others might be required of people (assignments and law). People assume responsibilities without much **conscious choice** (customs). People also assume responsibilities through some combination of consent, requirement, or without much conscious thought (appointment, occupation, citizenship, and moral principles).

C. Critical Thinking Exercise
Examining Responsibilities

Have students work with a study partner to complete the critical thinking exercise, "Examining Responsibilities," on pp. 122-123 of the text. With the class read the instructions for completing the exercise and review the questions. After students have completed their work, ask them to share their responses.

D. Concluding the Lesson

Have students draw a picture illustrating a responsibility another person has toward them. Ask students to explain the following:

- the source of that responsibility
- whether it was assumed voluntarily, required of the person, or assumed without much conscious thought
- what rewards and penalties might be associated with that responsibility

Have students display their illustrations for the class.

Using the Lesson

The activities suggested in "Using the Lesson" on p. 123 of the text reinforce or extend what students have learned about identifying sources of responsibility and how people assume responsibilities. You may have students complete these exercises individually or in small groups. Ask students to share their work with the class.

Lesson 3: How Can You Examine Responsibilities?

Lesson Overview

This lesson helps students apply what they have learned about responsibility to specific situations. Students examine the responsibilities in a manufacturer's **warranty**, in President Franklin D. Roosevelt's New Deal promises, in a court of law, and in a part-time job after school. This lesson also introduces students to a set of procedures, or "intellectual tools," useful in examining issues of responsibility.

Lesson Objectives

At the conclusion of this lesson, students should be able to do the following:

- identify and explain the sources of responsibilities in specific situations
- apply a set of procedures or intellectual tools useful in examining responsibilities in different situations

Preparation/Materials Required

Student text pp. 124-126

A copy for each student of the "Responsibility Study Chart" on p. 126 of the student text

Newspapers and/or newsmagazines for each group

Teaching Procedures

A. Introducing the Lesson

While you post the "Terms to Know" on the board, have students read "Purpose of Lesson" on p. 124 of the text.

B. Reading and Discussion
Responsibility's Rewards and Penalties

Have the class read "Responsibility's Rewards and Penalties" on p. 124 of the text. Ask students to examine the "Responsibility Study Chart" on p. 126 of the text. Discuss with the class the purpose and usefulness of intellectual tools in making decisions about responsibility. Refer to p. 6 of this guide for a discussion of intellectual tools.

C. Critical Thinking Exercise
Examining Responsibilities

Have students work with a study partner to complete the critical thinking exercise, "Examining Responsibilities," on pp. 124-125 of the text. The reading selections describe the responsibilities assumed by an appliance manufacturer, President Franklin D. Roosevelt, a judge in a court of law, and a student employee. Distribute a copy of the "Responsibility Study Chart" on p. 126 of the student text to each student. With the class read the instructions for completing the exercise. Review the questions in the study chart with the class. Allow time for students to complete their work. Ask students to share their responses.

D. Concluding the Lesson

Divide the class into groups of three to five students. Distribute newspapers and/or newsmagazines to each group. Ask the students to find articles that describe situations in which people fulfilled or failed to fulfill responsibilities. Ask students to identify the following:

- the responsibilities
- to whom the responsibilities are owed
- the sources of the responsibilities
- the rewards or penalties for fulfilling or not fulfilling them

Have students share their articles with the class.

Have the class re-read "Purpose of Lesson" on p. 124 of the text. Ask students to describe the extent to which they achieved the objectives of the lesson.

Using the Lesson

The activities in "Using the Lesson" on p. 126 of the text reinforce or extend what students have learned about identifying sources of responsibility, how people assume responsibilities, and rewards and penalties for fulfilling or not fulfilling responsibilities. Encourage students to use the "Responsibility Study Chart" when working on these activities. You may have students complete these exercises individually or in small groups. Ask students to share their work with the class.

This lesson concludes the study of Unit One, "What Is the Importance of Responsibility?" Have students write a summary in their journals of what they have learned about the following:

- responsibility
- the sources of responsibility
- how people assume responsibilities
- the rewards and penalties for fulfilling and not fulfilling responsibilities

They also may record questions about responsibility they still have and/or would like to explore.

Unit Two: What Might Be Some Benefits and Costs of Fulfilling Responsibilities?

Introduce **Unit Two: What Might Be Some Benefits and Costs of Fulfilling Responsibilities?** Explain that fulfilling responsibilities usually involves both benefits (advantages) and costs (disadvantages). It is often important to consider benefits and costs when deciding whether or not to take a particular responsibility or which responsibility to give priority to over others.

Direct attention to the illustration on p. 127 of the text. Ask students to respond to the question in the caption, "What might be some benefits and costs of working at the Snack Shack?" Record their responses on the board.

Have the class read "Purpose of Unit" on p. 127 of the text. Help students understand the use of the terms **benefits** and **costs** as advantages and disadvantages and the reasons for wanting to know the benefits and costs of fulfilling a responsibility. Ask students to list two things they expect to learn from their study of Unit Two. If students are keeping a journal during their study of this curriculum, they can record what they expect to learn.

Lesson 4: What Are the Consequences of Fulfilling Responsibility?

<table>
<tr><td>

Lesson Overview

This lesson helps students recognize the consequences of fulfilling responsibilities in specific situations. Students then learn to classify those consequences as **benefits** (advantages) or **costs** (disadvantages). During the critical thinking exercise, students analyze a situation in which a lifeguard reflects on the consequences of fulfilling the responsibilities of her job.

Lesson Objectives

At the conclusion of this lesson, students should be able to do the following:

- identify the consequences of fulfilling responsibility in specific situations
- classify those consequences as benefits or costs
- explain some of the most common benefits and costs of fulfilling responsibility

Preparation/Materials Required

Student text pp. 128-131

</td></tr>
</table>

Teaching Procedures

A. Introducing the Lesson

Ask students to identify a responsibility that interests them, but that they are not sure they wish to undertake. Responsibilities might include owning a pet or taking an after-school job. Record several of the responses on the board. For each response, ask students to describe the responsibility and the probable results of fulfilling it. Ask them to think about whether those results are advantages or disadvantages.

While you post the "Terms to Know" on the board, have students read "Purpose of Lesson" on p. 128 of the text.

B. Reading and Discussion
Benefits and Costs

Have the class read "Benefits and Costs" on pp. 128-129 of the text. Discuss the three sections of the reading with the class.

Discuss **benefits to others**. Post the following terms on the board:

- **predictability**
- **security**
- **efficiency**
- **fairness**
- **community spirit**

Ask students to describe the terms and to offer examples from their experience that illustrate each.

Discuss **benefits to the person fulfilling the responsibility**. Post the following terms on the board:

- **independence**
- **self-esteem**
- **acceptance and approval**
- **gains in knowledge, skill, and experience**
- **increased recognition, status, or payment**

Ask students to describe the terms and to offer examples from their experience that illustrate each.

Discuss **costs to the person fulfilling the responsibility**. Post the following terms on the board:

- **burdens**
- **sacrifice of other interests**
- **resentment**
- **fear of failure**
- **unfairness**

Ask students to describe the terms and to offer examples from their experience that illustrate each.

C. Critical Thinking Exercise
Examining Consequences of Fulfilling Responsibility

Have students work with a study partner to complete the critical thinking exercise, "Examining Consequences of Fulfilling Responsibility," on p. 130 of the text. With the class read the directions for completing the exercise. At the conclusion, ask students to share their work with the class.

D. Critical Thinking Exercise
Identifying and Classifying Consequences of Fulfilling Responsibilities

Have the class work in groups of three to five students to complete the critical thinking exercise, "Identifying and Classifying Consequences of Fulfilling Responsibilities," on pp. 130-131 of the text. With the class read the directions for completing the exercise. Review the questions in "Examining Responsibilities" on p. 131. After students have completed their work, ask them to share their responses with the class.

E. Concluding the Lesson

Direct attention to the illustration on p. 129 of the text. Ask students to identify the consequences of fulfilling responsibilities in this situation. Record their responses on the board. Ask students to determine which of the consequences are the following:

- benefits to others
- benefits to the person(s) fulfilling the responsibility
- costs to the person(s) fulfilling the responsibility

Have the class re-read "Purpose of Lesson" on p. 128 of the text. Ask students to describe the extent to which they achieved the objectives of the lesson.

Using the Lesson

The activities suggested in "Using the Lesson" on p. 131 of the text reinforce or extend what students have learned about benefits and costs of fulfilling responsibility. You may have students complete these exercises individually or in small groups. Ask students to share their work with the class.

Lesson 5:   How Can You Decide Whether the Benefits of Taking on Certain Responsibilities Outweigh the Costs?

Lesson Overview

This lesson provides students with additional practice in recognizing the consequences of fulfilling responsibilities and classifying those consequences as benefits or costs. During the lesson students role-play a **legislative hearing** to decide whether or not the state government should develop and maintain a wilderness park on donated land.

Lesson Objectives

At the conclusion of this lesson, students should be able to do the following:

- identify the consequences of assuming and fulfilling the responsibilities of developing and maintaining a wilderness park
- classify those consequences as benefits or costs
- explain different points of view regarding the relative importance of the benefits and costs

Preparation/Materials Required

Student text pp. 132-135

Optional: invite a community resource person such as a local political leader to the class

Teaching Procedures

A. Introducing the Lesson

While you post the "Terms to Know" on the board, have the class read "Purpose of Lesson" on p. 132 of the text.

B. Reading and Discussion
Evaluating the Relative Importance of Benefits and Costs

Have the class read "Evaluating the Relative Importance of Benefits and Costs" on p. 132 of the text. Help students understand the term **relative importance** and the reason people may have different views about the relative importance of the benefits and costs of fulfilling responsibilities in specific situations.

C. Critical Thinking Exercise
Weighing Benefits and Costs

This critical thinking exercise provides background information necessary for role-playing a legislative hearing. Have the class read "Weighing Benefits and Costs" on pp. 132-133 of the text. The selection, "The State Park Controversy," describes the possible consequences of a bill introduced in the state legislature to develop and maintain a wilderness park on land recently donated to the state. Discuss the following questions with the class:

- **What new responsibilities is the state considering?**

Students should recognize that the state is considering taking all the responsibilities inherent in developing and maintaining a large wilderness park

- **What would be the consequences of taking the responsibilities?**

Students should identify and describe the consequences of taking these responsibilities, including the following:

- the expenditure of large sums of money
- the problems involved in contracting or supervising the building of the planned facilities
- the need for related improvements such as a wider road
- damage to the natural environment
- increased access to the wilderness land for a greater number of people
- new jobs
- the creation of needed recreational facilities

- **Which consequences would be benefits? Which would be costs?**

Students should classify each of the consequences as benefits or costs and explain the reasons for their classifications.

D. Reading and Discussion
Preparing for and Conducting a Legislative Hearing

On the board post the following roles represented in the legislative hearing:

- Committee on Parks and Wildlife
- Citizens for Lower Taxes
- The Wildlife Coalition
- State Ranger's Union
- Citizens for Children's Outdoor Activities

Have the class read "Preparing for and Conducting a Legislative Hearing" on pp. 133-134 of the text. Review this section with the class and check for understanding of the process for participating in this activity. Also review the public hearing agenda on p. 133 with the class.

With the class read the instructions for preparing to participate in this activity, "Developing Group Presentations," on p. 134 and review the questions in this section. Assign students to each of the five roles you posted on the board. Ask students to read their group profiles on p. 135. Allow adequate time for the groups to respond to the questions and to prepare their presentations.

For more detailed instructions on conducting a legislative hearing, refer to p. 12 of this guide.

If you invited a community resource person to the class, ask him or her to help students prepare their presentations and to participate with the members of the Committee on Parks and Wildlife during the hearing. The community resource person should also participate in the concluding discussion.

E. Concluding the Lesson

At the conclusion of the legislative hearing, ask the members of the Committee on Parks and Wildlife to share their decision with the class on whether to recommend the bill as it is, to change it, or to vote against it. Ask the members of the committee to comment on which arguments presented were most persuasive. Were there any additional arguments that might have been made?

With the class discuss the relative importance each group placed on the benefits and costs of fulfilling responsibilities in this situation. Also discuss the usefulness of analyzing the consequences of fulfilling responsibilities when deciding whether or not to assume a particular responsibility.

Have the class re-read "Purpose of Lesson" on p. 132 of the text. Ask students to describe the extent to which they achieved the objectives of the lesson.

Using the Lesson

The activities suggested in "Using the Lesson" on p. 135 of the text reinforce or extend what students have learned about benefits and costs of fulfilling responsibility. You may have students complete these exercises individually or in small groups. Ask students to share their work with the class.

This lesson concludes the study of Unit Two, "What Might Be Some Benefits and Costs of Fulfilling Responsibilities?" Have students write a summary in their journals of what they have learned about the benefits and costs of fulfilling responsibilities.

Unit Three: How Should Conflicts Between Competing Responsibilities Be Resolved?

Introduce **Unit Three: How Should Conflicts Between Competing Responsibilities Be Resolved?** Remind students that people often face competing responsibilities. At these times we need to make reasonable decisions about which responsibilities we should fulfill and which values and interests we should pursue.

Explain that this unit is designed to increase their ability to make systematic and informed choices among competing responsibilities, values, and interests and to evaluate choices made by others. During their study of this unit, students will learn a procedure, or intellectual tools, that will assist them in this process. The first steps in the intellectual tools involve a review of what students learned in Units One and Two about identifying the following:

- responsibilities
- sources of those responsibilities
- related rewards and penalties for fulfillment or nonfulfillment
- probable benefits and costs of fulfilling particular responsibilities

Students learn additional considerations useful in making a decision regarding competing responsibilities, interests, and values. These considerations include the following:

- urgency
- relative importance
- time required
- resources available
- competing values and interests
- alternate solutions or compromises

After considering these factors, students develop and justify positions regarding the treatment of competing responsibilities, interests, and values.

Direct attention to the illustration on p. 136 of the student text. Ask students to identify the responsibilities shown in the picture. Ask students to respond to the question in the caption, "How can you decide which responsibilities to fulfill?"

Have the class read "Purpose of Unit" on p. 136 of the text. Ask students to list two things they expect to learn from their study of Unit Three.

Lesson 6: How Should One Choose Among Competing Responsibilities, Values, and Interests?

Lesson Overview

This lesson develops students' understanding of two kinds of conflicts that may arise in fulfilling responsibilities:

1. conflicts between competing responsibilities with no way of fulfilling them, at least not at the same time

2. conflicts among responsibilities and other values and interests

First students learn to identify values and interests. Then they examine two situations that illustrate the two kinds of conflicts that may arise in fulfilling responsibilities.

Lesson Objectives

At the conclusion of this lesson, students should be able to do the following:

- explain two kinds of conflicts that may arise in fulfilling responsibilities

- explain the terms **values** and **interests**

- identify various competing responsibilities, values, and interests in particular situations

- develop and support positions in situations where they must make choices among competing responsibilities, values, and interests

Preparation/Materials Required

Student text pp. 137-139

Teaching Procedures

A. Introducing the Lesson

Ask students to identify some situations in which they have had more responsibilities to fulfill than they could manage. Post some competing responsibilities that they describe on the board. Ask students to describe how they decided which responsibilities to fulfill and which not to fulfill. What other options might have been available in these situations?

While you post the "Terms to Know" on the board, have the class read "Purpose of Lesson" on p. 137 of the student text.

B. Reading and Discussion
What kinds of conflicts may arise in fulfilling responsibilities?

Have the class read "What kinds of conflicts may arise in fulfilling responsibilities?" on pp. 137-138 of the text. Ask students to identify the two common types of conflicts that may arise when people have to make choices about fulfilling responsibilities. Record their responses on the board.

Help students understand that in some situations two or more responsibilities may be in conflict because a person cannot fulfill them, at least not at the same time. Ask students to illustrate this kind of conflict by citing examples from their experience.

Also help students understand that in other situations there might be a conflict among responsibilities and other values and interests. Direct attention to the illustration on p. 137 of the text. Ask students to respond to the two questions in the caption:

- What values are shown in this picture?
- What are some of your values?

Ask students to explain the terms **values** and **interests** and to suggest examples from the reading or their experience. Ask students to illustrate the conflict among responsibilities and other values and interests by citing examples from their experience.

Help students understand that sometimes in deciding which responsibility to fulfill, one may have to sacrifice a particular value or interest. Sometimes a person may decide not to fulfill a responsibility because some other value or interest is more important.

C. Critical Thinking Exercise
Examining Competing Responsibilities, Values, and Interests

Have students work with a study partner to complete the critical thinking exercise, "Examining Competing Responsibilities, Values, and Interests," on p. 138 of the student text. Read the instructions for completing the exercise with the class and review the questions in "Identifying Competing Responsibilities, Values, and Interests." When responding to question number 1, encourage students to identify the following:

- the responsibilities
- the source or sources of the responsibilities
- the rewards for fulfilling them
- the penalties for not fulfilling them
- the benefits and costs of fulfilling the responsibilities

You may want to post these items on the board as a reminder of the procedures students learned in Units One and Two. These items are the first part of the procedure, or intellectual tools, for deciding among competing responsibilities, values, and interests. Students will learn the second part of the procedure in Lesson 7.

After students have completed the exercise, ask them to share their responses with the class.

D. Concluding the Lesson

Have the class re-read "Purpose of Lesson" on p. 137. Ask students to describe the extent to which they achieved the objectives of the lesson.

Using the Lesson

The activities suggested in "Using the Lesson" on p. 139 of the text reinforce or extend what students have learned about the kinds of conflicts that may arise in fulfilling responsibilities, identifying values and interests, and analyzing competing responsibilities, values, and interests. You may have students complete these exercises individually or in small groups. When assigning these exercises, encourage students to apply the procedures they have learned for analyzing responsibilities. Ask students to share their work with the class.

Lesson 7: How Can You Decide Among Competing Responsibilities?

<table>
<tr><td>

Lesson Overview

Students learn a set of considerations used to make decisions about competing responsibilities. These considerations form part of the procedure, or intellectual tools, useful in analyzing and evaluating an issue involving competing responsibilities, values, and interests. During the critical thinking exercise, students apply the procedure in an imaginary situation to decide whether money in a savings account should be loaned to a friend or used to purchase concert tickets.

Lesson Objectives

At the conclusions of this lesson, students should be able to do the following:

- explain a set of considerations useful for choosing among competing responsibilities, values, and interests

- apply a procedure, including the set of considerations, useful in analyzing and evaluating an issue involving competing responsibilities, values, and interests

- arrive at a decision on such an issue and explain the basis for that decision

Preparation/Materials Required

Student text pp. 140-144

A copy for each student of the "Intellectual Tool Chart for Deciding Among Responsibilities" on p. 144 of the student text

</td></tr>
</table>

Teaching Procedures

A. Introducing the Lesson

While you post the "Terms to Know" on the board, have students read "Purpose of Lesson" on p. 140 of the text.

B. Reading and Discussion

Considerations Useful in Deciding Among Competing Responsibilities

Post the following terms on the board:

1. urgency
2. relative importance
3. time required
4. resources available
5. competing values and interests
6. alternative solutions or compromises

Explain that these six ideas can help people make difficult decisions about carrying out responsibilities and protecting other values and interests.

Have the class read "Considerations Useful in Deciding Among Competing Responsibilities" on pp. 140-143 of the text. At the conclusion, ask students to describe each of the six considerations. Record their responses next to the corresponding terms that you posted previously on the board. Ask students to identify the competing responsibilities cited in each example. Then ask students to respond to the questions that follow each example.

You may want the class to share the responsibility for reading and learning this material. If so, divide the class into six groups and assign each group one of the six considerations in the reading. Ask each group to do the following:

- describe their consideration to the class

- explain the example that illustrates that consideration

- identify the competing responsibilities cited in the example

- give their responses to the questions that follow each example

At the conclusion, help students understand that even though only two or three of these considerations might be important, they should apply all six to ensure that they have not overlooked a relevant consideration.

C. Critical Thinking Exercise
Deciding Among Competing Responsibilities

Have the class work in groups of three to five students to complete the critical thinking exercise, "Deciding Among Competing Responsibilities," on p. 143 of the text. The reading selection, "Short of Funds," describes competing responsibilities when Stacey wants to purchase tickets to a rock concert but has promised to loan the money to a friend for needed automobile repairs.

With the class read the instructions for completing the exercise and review the questions in the "What do you think?" section on p. 143. To each student distribute a copy of the "Intellectual Tool Chart for Deciding Among Responsibilities" on p. 144 of the student text. Allow adequate time for students to complete their chart and to respond to the questions on p. 143.

D. Concluding the Lesson

After groups have completed the critical thinking exercise, ask students to share their responses to the "What do you think?" questions. Encourage students to use the information on their intellectual tool chart to support their positions on which competing responsibility should be fulfilled.

Ask students to evaluate the usefulness of this procedure for deciding among competing responsibilities.

Have the class re-read "Purpose of Lesson" on p. 140 of the text. Ask them to describe the extent to which they achieved the objectives of the lesson.

Using the Lesson

The activities suggested in "Using the Lesson" on p. 143 of the text reinforce or extend what students have learned about the considerations and the procedure useful in deciding among competing responsibilities. You may have students complete these exercises individually or in small groups. When assigning these exercises, encourage students to apply the procedures they have learned for analyzing responsibilities. Ask students to share their work with the class.

Lesson 8: How Would You Deal With the Conflicting Responsibilities in This Situation?

Lesson Overview

Students gain additional practice in analyzing and evaluating situations involving conflicting responsibilities, values, and interests. The critical thinking exercise describes an emergency room situation in which a doctor must decide whether or not to treat a seriously injured and unconscious patient. The patient's wallet contains a card requesting that in case of injury medical treatment be withheld for religious reasons. Students apply the intellectual tools and then present and support positions on how they might resolve the **dilemma**.

Lesson Objectives

At the conclusion of this lesson, students should be able to do the following:

- apply a given procedure and a set of considerations to analyze and evaluate a situation
- develop and support a position on the way the conflict should be resolved

Preparation/Materials Required

Student text pp. 145-146

Optional: Invite a member of the medical profession to the class to work with students in developing and supporting positions on this issue

---

Teaching Procedures

A. Introducing the Lesson

Direct attention to the photograph on p. 145 of the student text. Ask students to respond to the question in the caption, "How can emergency situations create conflicting responsibilities?"

While you post the "Terms to Know" on the board, have the class read "Purpose of Lesson" on p. 145 of the text.

B. Reading and Discussion
Resolving a Dilemma

Have the class read "Resolving a Dilemma" on p. 145 of the text. During the discussion, help students understand the nature of a **dilemma**: in certain situations a person has a responsibility to do something and also a responsibility not to do it. Ask students to identify from their experience a dilemma they or someone they know has had to resolve.

C. Critical Thinking Exercise
Deciding Among Conflicting Responsibilities

Have students work with a study partner to complete the critical thinking exercise, "Deciding Among Conflicting Responsibilities," on pp. 145-146 of the text. The reading selection, "The Emergency," describes an emergency room dilemma in which a doctor must decide whether to administer treatment according to the **Hippocratic Oath** or withhold that treatment to respect a seriously injured and unconscious patient's freedom of religion. With the class read the instructions for completing the exercise and review the questions in "Examining the Situation" on p. 146.

If you have invited a person from the medical profession to class, ask that person to help students formulate responses to the questions in "Examining the Situation." At the conclusion, ask the resource person to respond to the way students developed and supported their position in this situation. Also ask the resource person to share with the class the way he or she has resolved similar conflicting responsibilities.

The chart on the next page offers some responses students might give to questions 1-10 in "Examining the Situation."

Intellectual Tool Chart for Deciding Among Responsibilities

Question	Responsibility 1:	Responsibility 2:
1. What are the doctor's responsibilities?	To try to save patient's life	To respect patient's wishes not to operate or render treatment without the patient's consent
2. What are the **sources** of those responsibilities?	Hippocratic Oath, occupation, law, moral principles	Assignment (through card in wallet), moral principles, law
3. What might be some **rewards** for fulfilling the responsibilities? What might be some **penalties** for not fulfilling the responsibilities?	(Reward) income, respect and approval from others, self-satisfaction (Penalty) loss of job or license to practice, guilt	(Reward) consistent with own beliefs, patient may survive (Penalty) disapproval of others, guilt, possible lawsuit by family
4. What are the probable **consequences** of fulfillment? Which are **benefits**? Which are **costs**?	(Benefit) patient may get well (Cost) doctor may feel anxiety about not following patient's wishes, doctor might be sued by family	(Benefit) patient's wishes will be honored (Cost) patient may die
5. How **urgent** is each responsibility?	Very urgent, patient near death	Difficult to say—within scheme of religious belief, appears urgent not to interfere with spiritual healing process
6. What is the **relative importance** of each responsibility?	Very important to the doctor	Very important to the patient
7. What amount of **time** would be **required** to fulfill each responsibility?	Not significant except in relation to emergency	Not significant except in relation to emergency
8. What **resources** are **required** to fulfill each responsibility?	Not significant. Necessary resources appear to be available	Questionable. Is a member of the church available?
9. What other **values** or **interests** are involved?	Religious freedom	Religious freedom
10. What **alternative solutions** are possible?	Try to get approval by family Try to get court order approving surgery	

D. Concluding the Lesson

Ask students to share their responses to questions number 1-10 in "Examining the Situation" on p. 146. Have a spokesperson from each pair present their position in response to question number 11, "What should Dr. Green do? Why?" Encourage students to support their position with reasoning formulated during analysis and evaluation of the dilemma.

Ask students to evaluate the usefulness of the intellectual tools for developing and supporting a position among competing responsibilities.

Using the Lesson

The activities suggested in "Using the Lesson" on p. 146 of the text reinforce or extend what students have learned about using intellectual tools to make decisions about situations involving competing responsibilities. You may have students complete these exercises individually or in small groups. When assigning these exercises, encourage students to apply the procedures they have learned for analyzing responsibilities. Ask students to share their work.

Lesson 9: Which Responsibilities Should the Representative Fulfill?

Lesson Overview

Students are provided with additional practice in analyzing and evaluating situations involving conflicting responsibilities, values, and interests. Students role-play a public hearing before Representative Martin of the United States House of Representatives who wants to hear from her constituents before deciding whether or not to support a bill closing several Air Force bases including one important to the economy of her state. Students complete an intellectual tool chart and then present and support positions on whether or not Representative Martin should support the bill.

Lesson Objectives

At the conclusion of this lesson, students should be able to do the following:

- apply a given procedure and a set of considerations to analyze and evaluate a situation
- develop and support a position on a decision in this situation

Preparation/Materials Required

Student text pp. 147-150

A copy for each student of "Representative Martin's Chart of Considerations" on p. 150 of the student text

Optional: Invite an elected official to the class to help students prepare their presentations and to participate in the hearing

Teaching Procedures

A. Introducing the Lesson

Direct attention to the illustration on p. 148 of the text. Ask students to respond to the question in the caption, "What are the responsibilities of elected officials?" During the discussion, help students understand that members of Congress frequently face conflicting demands because they are responsible simultaneously to the following:

- their constituents
- their supporters
- their political party
- the people of their state
- the nation

Follow the discussion by directing attention to the illustration on p. 147. Ask students to respond to the question in the caption, "How can elected officials resolve conflicting responsibilities to their constituents?"

Have the class read "Purpose of Lesson" on p. 147 of the text.

B. Critical Thinking Exercise
Taking and Defending a Position

This critical thinking exercise is a hypothetical situation that involves the class in role-playing a public hearing before a member of the United States House of Representatives. Have the class read "Taking and Defending a Position" on pp. 147-149 of the text. The reading selection, "Should the Air Force Base Be Closed?" describes the post-Cold War era during which the United States decided to reduce the size and cost of the military. After the President approved a list of base closures, he sent the bill to Congress. Included in the bill was an Air Force base that was a very large employer in Representative Martin's state.

While students complete their reading, post the following roles on the board:

- Representative Martin and her staff
- the Democratic Club
- Association of Aged and Retired Persons
- retired army officers
- the Banker's Association
- people who live near the base
- people who favor reduction of defense spending

Discuss the reading with the class, making sure students understand the conflicting demands on Representative Martin. Ask student to identify Representative Martin's conflicting responsibilities, values, and interests. Record their responses on the board.

Divide the class into seven groups and assign each group one of the roles you posted on the board. Read "Developing and Presenting Group Positions" on p. 149 with the class. Make sure students understand the instructions for participating in the role-play. To each student distribute a copy of "Representative Martin's Chart of Considerations" on p. 150 of the student text. Allow adequate time for students to develop a position on whether or not Representative Martin should support the proposed bill. Conduct the role-play. For more detailed instructions on conducting a public hearing, refer to p. 12 of this guide.

If you invited an elected official to the class, ask him or her to work with the students to prepare their positions. Also ask the resource person to listen to the presentations and to participate in the concluding discussion with the class. Encourage the resource person to share experiences with the class similar to the one presented in this situation.

C. Concluding the Lesson

After conducting the role-play, ask Representative Martin and her staff to divulge whether or not the congresswoman will support the bill. Ask the group to identify the arguments presented that most influenced the decision. Ask students to share their personal views on this issue. Discuss the usefulness of using intellectual tools to develop and support a position on this issue.

Have the class re-read "Purpose of Lesson" on p. 147 of the text. Ask students to describe the extent to which they achieved the objectives of the lesson.

Using the Lesson

The activities suggested in "Using the Lesson" on p. 149 of the text reinforce or extend what students have learned about using intellectual tools to make decisions about situations involving competing responsibilities. You may have students complete these exercises individually or in small groups. When assigning these exercises, encourage students to apply the procedures they have learned for analyzing responsibilities. Ask students to share their work with the class.

This lesson concludes the study of Unit Three, "How Should Conflicts Between Competing Responsibilities Be Resolved?" Have students write a summary in their journals of what they have learned about the considerations and the set of procedures, or intellectual tools, for analyzing and evaluating conflicts among competing responsibilities, values, and interests.

Unit Four: Who Should Be Considered Responsible?

Introduce **Unit Four: Who Should Be Considered Responsible?** Remind students that during the first three units of this curriculum, they explored an aspect of responsibility concerned with the duty or obligation of a person or persons to do something or to refrain from doing something in a particular situation.

Explain that Unit Four explores another way people use the concept of responsibility. During the next few lessons they will learn a set of considerations and procedures useful in deciding who is responsible for something that has happened in terms of being answerable, accountable, or deserving of credit. It is useful to determine responsibility for the following purposes:

- to reward an individual or group for a positive act
- to hold an individual or group answerable for a wrong or injury
- to use the knowledge to guide future actions

Direct attention to the illustration on p. 151 of the student text. Ask students to identify the persons responsible for the events shown in the picture. Ask students to respond to the question in the caption, "Why is it important to decide who should be considered responsible for an event or situation?"

Have the class read "Purpose of Unit" on p. 151 of the text. Ask students to list two things they expect to learn from their study of Unit Four. If students are keeping journals during their study of this curriculum, they can record their responses in their journals.

Lesson 10: Why Might We Want to Decide Who Is Responsible?

> ## Lesson Overview
>
> Students examine reasons people want to determine who is responsible for a particular situation or event. Students learn that people may want to reward someone for something good they have done, to penalize a person for a wrong or injury they have caused, or to guide actions in the future. Students respond to hypothetical situations that help them understand the importance and difficulties of deciding who should be held responsible for a particular situation or event.
>
> ## Lesson Objectives
>
> At the conclusion of this lesson, students should be able to do the following:
>
> - explain three reasons for wanting to determine who should be considered responsible for a particular situation or event
> - develop and justify positions regarding who should be considered responsible in two hypothetical situations
>
> ## Preparation/Materials Required
>
> Student text pp. 152-154
>
> Newspapers and/or newsmagazines for the class

Teaching Procedures

A. Introducing the Lesson

Ask students to give examples of times they had to determine who was responsible for a particular situation or event. Why did they want or need to make such determinations? What did they consider in making their decisions?

Have the class read "Purpose of Lesson" on p. 152 of the student text.

B. Reading and Discussion

Why do we want to be able to determine responsibility?

Post the following terms on the board: **reward, penalize, guide.**

Have the class read "Why do we want to be able to determine responsibility?" on pp. 152-153 of the text. Ask students to explain the three reasons for wanting to determine who is responsible for a situation or event and to illustrate each reason with examples from the reading or their experiences.

C. Critical Thinking Exercise

Deciding Who Should Be Held Responsible

Have students work with a study partner to complete the critical thinking exercise, "Deciding Who Should Be Held Responsible," on pp. 153-154 of the text. The first selection, "The Collision," briefly describes an automobile accident. The second selection, "Parkland," describes a successful campaign that got voters to authorize the purchase, development, and maintenance of a 275 acre park. Read the instructions for completing the exercise with the class and review the questions in both "What do you think?" sections on p. 153 and p. 154. Ask students to share their responses with the class. Discuss the reason that it was difficult to determine who was responsible in each situation with the class.

D. Concluding the Lesson

Distribute newspapers and/or newsmagazines to the class. Have students work with a study partner to locate articles illustrating situations in which someone is responsible for an achievement, a wrong, or an injury. Have the students share their articles with the class.

Have the class re-read "Purpose of Lesson" on p. 152 of the text. Ask students to describe the extent to which they achieved the objectives of the lesson.

> ## Using the Lesson
>
> The activities suggested in "Using the Lesson" on p. 154 of the text reinforce or extend what students have learned about why people want to determine who is responsible for a situation or event. You may have students complete these exercise individually or in small groups. Ask students to share their work with the class.

Lesson 11: What Intellectual Tools Are Useful in Determining Responsibility?

Lesson Overview

This lesson introduces students to a procedure, or the use of intellectual tools, to help determine who should be considered responsible for an achievement or a wrongdoing. During the critical thinking exercise, students apply the procedure to determine who was responsible for an accident in the school cafeteria.

Lesson Objectives

At the conclusion of this lesson, students should be able to do the following:

- use the intellectual tools to determine who is responsible for a situation or event

- apply the intellectual tools to make a decision about a hypothetical situation

Preparation/Materials Required

Student text pp. 155-158

Teaching Procedures

A. Introducing the Lesson

While you post the "Terms to Know" on the board, have the class read "Purpose of Lesson" on p. 155 of the text.

B. Reading and Discussion

What intellectual tools are useful in determining responsibility?

Post on the board, or make a transparency of the seven steps of the intellectual tools used to determine who is responsible for a situation or event:

1. What is the **event** or **situation** for which someone might be considered responsible?

2. Who are **the people involved** who might be considered responsible for what happened?

3. How might each person be considered to have **caused** the event or situation?

4. Did the person's conduct violate or fail to fulfill a **duty** or **obligation** he or she had?

5. What was the individual's **state of mind** when he or she caused something to happen?

   a. **intent**

   b. **recklessness**

   c. **carelessness**

   d. **knowledge of probable consequences**

6. Did the person or persons have **control** over their actions? Did they have a **choice** to do something other than what they did?

7. Did the person or persons have more **important values, interests,** or **responsibilities** that caused them to act as they did?

Have the class read "What intellectual tools are useful in determining responsibility?" on pp. 155-158 of the text. Discuss each step in the procedure with the class. Ask students to explain the step and to offer examples from the reading or their experience that illustrate that step. At the conclusion, help students understand that steps 1-3 are used to make decisions about who should be considered responsible for an achievement. All seven steps are used when determining responsibility for some wrongdoing.

You may want the class to share responsibility for learning the steps in this procedure. If so, divide the class into seven groups and assign each group one of the steps. Ask each group to explain its assigned step to the class and to illustrate that step with examples from the reading.

C. Critical Thinking Exercise
Applying Intellectual Tools to Determine Responsibility

Have students work with a study partner to complete the critical thinking exercise, "Applying Intellectual Tools to Determine Responsibility," on p. 158 of the text. Allow adequate time for students to analyze the situation and to decide who should be considered responsible for the accident in the school cafeteria.

D. Concluding the Lesson

Ask students to share their responses to the critical thinking exercise with the class. Ask students who should be considered responsible and why. Ask students to explain some of the difficulties they encountered in determining responsibility in this situation.

Using the Lesson

The activities suggested in "Using the Lesson" on p. 158 of the text reinforce or extend what students have learned about using a procedure to determine who is responsible for a situation or event. You may help students invite an attorney or judge to the class or organize a field experience to a courtroom. You may assign these activities as individual or small group exercises. If you do, ask students to share their experiences with the class.

Lesson 12: Who Should Be Held Responsible for This Accident?

Lesson Overview

This lesson provides students with an opportunity to apply a specific situation to the procedure, or intellectual tools, they learned in Lesson 11. During the critical thinking exercise students analyze and evaluate the actions of several persons to determine who was responsible for an industrial accident that resulted in costly medical expenses to the company's health insurer.

Lesson Objectives

At the conclusion of this lesson, students should be able to do the following:

- explain the reason one would want to determine who was responsible in a particular event or situation

- apply a procedure to analyze and evaluate information gathered in a particular event or situation

- develop and support a position on who should be considered responsible for the event or situation

Preparation/Materials Required

Student text pp. 159-161

A copy for each student of the "Intellectual Tool Chart for Deciding Who Is Responsible" on p. 161 of the student text

Teaching Procedures

A. Introducing the Lesson

Direct attention to the illustration on p. 159 of the text. Ask students to respond to the question in the caption, "Why might it be important to determine responsibility for an accident?" Remind students of the reasons one would want to determine who is responsible for a situation or event (reward, penalize, or guide actions in the future). Help students understand that in a situation involving an accident one may want to impose penalties or make the responsible person(s) compensate for the damages. Another reason for wanting to know who is responsible is to guide actions in the future. Safety is an important interest and knowing who is responsible for an accident can help minimize or eliminate potentially hazardous conditions.

Have the class read "Purpose of Lesson" on p. 159 of the text.

B. Critical Thinking Exercise
Taking Positions on Responsibility

Have the class work in groups of three to five students to complete the critical thinking exercise, "Taking Positions on Responsibility," on pp. 159-160 of the text. The reading selection, "An Accident on the Job," describes the information gathered by a health insurance investigator following an accident at Beamer's Carpentry Shop. With the class read the instructions for completing the exercise. Distribute a copy to each student of the "Intellectual Tool Chart for

Deciding Who Is Responsible" on p. 161 of the student text. Review the questions on the study chart and the questions in the "What do you think?" section on p. 160.

Instruct each group to select a spokesperson and a recorder. Explain that groups need not reach consensus and may report majority and minority opinions or explain the reason they cannot make a recommendation in this situation. Further, students can assign responsibility for the accident to a single individual or distribute it among two or more individuals.

A sample completed chart on the next page is included as a guide for discussion. You also should accept other reasonable responses to the questions on the chart.

C. Concluding the Lesson

After groups have completed their work, have the spokespersons for each group make a brief presentation of the group's position. After all positions have been presented, conduct a class discussion evaluating various positions.

Ask students to vote on which position they favor to determine the class' preference. After the vote, explain that situations calling for determination of responsibility can be very complex and that sometimes important information may be missing. Nevertheless, people must make decisions on these kinds of problems.

Conclude the lesson by asking the students why it is important to determine who should be held responsible in this situation. Also ask students to evaluate the usefulness of the intellectual tools in helping decide who was responsible.

Using the Lesson

The activities suggested in "Using the Lesson" on p. 160 of the text reinforce or extend what students have learned about using a procedure to determine who is responsible for a situation or event. You may assign these activities as individual or small group exercises. Ask students to share their experiences with the class.

Intellectual Tool Chart for Deciding Who Is Responsible

	James Olson	Nick Greeley	Bill Beamer	Grace del Campo
1. What is the event or situation in question?	The injury to James Olson's arm			
2. Who are the persons who might be considered responsible?	James Olson	Nick Greeley	Bill Beamer	Grace del Campo
3. How might each person be considered to have **caused** the event or situation?	Contributed to his injuries by not using blade guard	Contributed to accident by backing forklift into table saw	Contributed to accident by not bolting down table saw	Contributed to accident by not inspecting table saw
4. What **duty** or **obligation**, if any, did the person's conduct violate or fail to fulfill?	To use due care in operating the table saw; to follow the company rule requiring the blade guard to be used	To use due care in operating the forklift; to follow the doctor's instruction not to return to work that day	To provide a safe work place for his employees; to bolt the saw down according to installation instructions from the manufacturer	To inspect each piece of machinery sold to ensure that it was correctly installed
5. What was the person's **state of mind**? Consider: ■ Intent ■ Recklessness ■ Carelessness or negligence ■ Knowledge of probable consequences	Chose not to use blade guard to protect himself from risk of injury. If decision was justified in light of experience and efficiency, conduct was not negligent; otherwise, conduct was careless or negligent	Recklessly or negligently chose to ignore doctor's advice and operate dangerous equipment while medicated; was aware of probable consequences	Negligently failed to bolt saw down; may not have been aware of probable consequences, but arguably should have been	Negligently postponed inspection; was aware of probable consequences
6. Did the person lack **control**? Could he or she have acted differently? Explain your answer.	Had choice	Lacked choice after he fell asleep but not before	Had choice	Had choice
7. What important **values, interests,** or **responsibilities,** if any, excuse the person's conduct?	He claimed efficiency and speed were increased by not using blade guard	Perhaps could not afford to miss a day's work and lose a day's pay	None apparent	None; simply wanted to leave for vacation

Lesson 13: Who Should Be Considered Responsible for This Achievement?

Lesson Overview

Students get additional practice in applying the procedure, or intellectual tools, to determine responsibility for a situation or event. The critical thinking exercise describes a situation in which many people contributed time, skills, and money to construct affordable housing for homeless senior citizens in their community. Students must decide who should receive an award for this positive achievement.

Lesson Objectives

At the conclusion of this lesson, students should be able to do the following:

- identify the person(s) or groups involved in the situation who might be considered responsible for a positive achievement

- apply a procedure to analyze and evaluate information in a particular event or situation

- develop and support a position on who should be rewarded for the event or situation

Preparation/Materials Required

Student text pp. 162-164

A copy for each student of the "Intellectual Tool Chart for Deciding Who Is Responsible" on p. 161 of the student text

Teaching Procedures

A. Introducing the Lesson

Have the class read "Purpose of Lesson" on p. 162 of the text.

B. Critical Thinking Exercise
Deciding Responsibility

Have the class read the critical thinking exercise, "Deciding Responsibility," on pp. 162-163 of the text. The selection, "The Senior Citizen's Home," describes the way Maria's letter to the school paper inspired other high school students to do something about the problem of homeless senior citizens in their community. As a result, both students and adults donated their time, skills, and financial resources to build low-cost apartments for senior citizens.

After students have completed their reading, ask them to respond to question number 1 in the "What do you think?" section on p. 164. Encourage students to identify all the individuals and groups who contributed to the senior citizens' apartments. Record their responses on the board.

Have the class work in groups of three to five students. Instruct the groups to select a spokesperson and a recorder. Review question number 2 in the "What do you think?" section.

Distribute a copy to each student of the "Intellectual Tool Chart for Deciding Who Is Responsible" on p. 161 of the student text. Review the steps on the chart and ask students to decide which ones are important in deciding who is responsible in this particular situation. Most likely they will suggest steps number 1-3. You may also suggest other factors students might consider in assigning credit for a positive achievement such as the time, labor, money, leadership, or creative ideas that people contributed. Allow time for group discussion.

C. Concluding the Lesson

After students have completed their work, ask the spokesperson in each group to present his or her group's decisions to the class. Ask other members of the group to explain the reasons for the decisions.

Conduct a class vote to determine which person(s) or groups students consider to be most responsible, second most responsible, and third most responsible for the achievement.

To conclude the lesson, ask students to identify some difficulties they encountered in reaching a decision. What additional information might have been helpful? Ask students to evaluate the usefulness of the intellectual tools in analyzing this situation.

Lesson 14: Who Should Be Held Responsible for the King's Murder?

Lesson Overview

This is the concluding lesson in the study of responsibility. It provides students with an opportunity to apply what they have learned about using intellectual tools to determine who is responsible for a situation or event. In the critical thinking exercise, students role-play criminal defense attorneys. The activity is based on William Shakespeare's *Macbeth*. After hearing the arguments, the class decides whether responsibility for the murder of King Duncan belongs to Macbeth, Lady Macbeth, the king's guards, or the three witches in the play.

Lesson Objectives

At the conclusion of this lesson, students should be able to do the following:

■ apply a procedure to analyze and evaluate information in a particular event or situation

■ develop and support a position regarding who should be responsible for the event or situation

Preparation/Materials Required

Student text pp. 165-167

A copy for each student of the "Intellectual Tool Chart for Deciding Who Is Responsible" on p. 167 of the student text

Optional: Invite an attorney or judge to the class to work with the students to evaluate the situation in this lesson and to participate in the role-play activity

Teaching Procedures

A. Introducing the Lesson

Have the class read "Purpose of Lesson" on p. 165 of the text.

B. Critical Thinking Exercise
Deciding Responsibility for a Murder

This critical thinking exercise provides the background information for role-playing criminal defense attorneys later in the lesson. Have the class read "Deciding Responsibility for Murder" on pp. 165-166 of the text. The reading selection, "The King Is Dead," is based on Shakespeare's *Macbeth* and describes the events leading to the murder of King Duncan.

After students have completed the reading, distribute a copy to each student of the "Intellectual Tool Chart for Deciding Who Is Responsible" on p. 167 of the student text. You may want students to work with a study partner to complete the chart.

After students complete their analysis of this situation, ask each of them to write his or her responses to the questions in the "What do you think?" section on p. 166. Do not ask students to share their responses at this time. This may be done during the concluding discussion following the role-play.

C. Critical Thinking Exercise
Role-Playing Criminal Defense Attorneys

With the class read "Role-Playing Criminal Defense Attorneys" on p. 166 of the text. Check for understanding of the instructions for participating in the role-play. Be sure students understand the role of a criminal defense attorney in a court of law.

Divide the class into teams representing the following:

- Macbeth
- Lady Macbeth
- the King's Guards
- the Three Witches

Instruct the groups to select a spokesperson to present their arguments to the class. Allow time for students to prepare. Encourage them to use the information from their study charts.

Have the spokesperson for each group present his or her group's arguments to the class. You may want to establish some time limits for the presentations.

D. Concluding the Lesson

At the conclusion of the presentations, direct the discussion to the questions in the "What do you think?" section on p. 166. During the discussion, remind the class that it could be argued that each of the four parties in the story have to a greater or lesser degree some responsibility for the king's murder. There are also plausible arguments on behalf of each as to the reason that party should be exonerated. The strength of

student responses does not rest on the position taken, but on how well the position is supported by sound reasoning and the use of the information in the "Intellectual Tool Chart for Deciding Who Is Responsible."

Ask students to examine their individual responses to the questions in the "What do you think?" section completed earlier in the lesson. Did anyone change his or her mind about who was responsible for the murder? If so, what influenced the change?

Using the Lesson

The activities suggested in "Using the Lesson" on p. 166 of the text reinforce or extend what students have learned about using a procedure to determine who is responsible for a situation or event. You may assign these activities as individual or small group exercises. Ask students to share their experiences with the class.

This lesson concludes the study of Unit Four, "Who Should Be Considered Responsible?" Have students write in their journals a summary of what they have learned about the considerations and the set of procedures, or intellectual tools, for deciding who is responsible for a situation or event.

Concluding the Responsibility Curriculum

This concludes the study of the Responsibility curriculum. It will be valuable to both you and your students to reflect on and evaluate the total experience with this section of *Foundations of Democracy*, including the content and the instruction methods.

Distribute a copy of "Reflecting on Your Experience" on p. 28 of this guide to each student. Remind students that they should not only reflect on and evaluate their experiences, but also those of the class. Have students share their responses with the class.

The Justice Curriculum

Introduce the Justice curriculum. Begin by reminding students that it is almost impossible to read a newspaper or watch a television program without encountering an instance of claimed injustice or unfairness in the treatment of a particular individual or group; in the distribution of certain goods, resources, or burdens; or in the trial of an alleged lawbreaker. Ask students to offer examples from their experience of someone or some group being treated fairly or unfairly. Ask them to explain what they think might have been fair or unfair in those situations.

Direct attention to the photograph on p. 170 of the student text. Ask students to describe the national issues of justice Dr. Martin Luther King, Jr. raised when he led the 1963 Civil Rights March on Washington. Ask students to identify issues of justice in their state or local community.

Have the class read the "Introduction" on p. 170 of the text. Ask students to identify some of the fundamental political and legal documents that demonstrate the historical commitment of our society to the pursuit of justice. Ask students to define the term **justice**. Justice, as the term is used in these materials, means roughly the same thing as **fairness**. Explain that in this study of justice the class will examine and make decisions about issues of justice in a number of specific situations. Explain that they will learn to apply several sets of "intellectual tools" to different types of problems of justice. These tools will help them deal with issues of justice in a thoughtful, reasoned manner. For a detailed description of intellectual tools, please see p. 6 of this guide.

Unit One: What Is Justice?

Introduce **Unit One: What Is Justice?** Explain that in this brief introductory unit the class will discuss issues of justice to better understand the relevance of the subject to their daily lives and how justice pertains to common issues in their communities, state, nation, and the world.

Direct attention to the illustrations on p. 171 of the text. Ask students to respond to the question in the caption, "What issues of fairness or justice are shown in these pictures?" Conclude the discussion by asking students to offer reasons that it might be important to study issues of justice.

Have students read "Purpose of Unit" on p. 171 of the text. Ask students to list three things they expect to learn from their study of Unit One. If students are keeping a journal during their study of this curriculum, they can record their list in their journals. Review these journal notations at the conclusion of the study of justice. Repeat this activity during the introductions to Units Two, Three, and Four.

Lesson 1: Why Divide Issues of Justice into Three Categories?

Lesson Overview

In this introductory lesson students first read and then discuss three situations that raise issues of **distributive**, **corrective**, and **procedural justice**. Students learn the definitions of these categories of justice and complete an exercise classifying situations according to the issue(s) of justice each raises. Students also develop and support positions on the fairness or unfairness of the issues. Finally, they identify situations from their experiences that represent the three categories of justice.

Lesson Objectives

At the conclusion of this lesson, students should be able to do the following:

- describe distributive, corrective, and procedural justice
- classify situations that raise issues of distributive, corrective, or procedural justice
- explain the usefulness of classifying issues of justice in this way
- describe situations they have experienced or observed that represent the three categories of justice

Preparation/Materials Required

Student text pp. 172-175

Newspapers and/or newsmagazines, at least one for each group of three students

Teaching Procedures

A. Introducing the Lesson

Ask students to recall situations in which they have used or heard others use the phrase, "that's not fair!" Record their responses on the board. Explain that these situations demonstrate the different categories of justice they will learn in this lesson. You may want to leave the list on the board and have the students classify the situations after they learn to identify each category of justice.

While you post the "Terms to Know" on the board, have students read "Purpose of Lesson" on p. 172 of the text.

B. Critical Thinking Exercise
Examining Issues of Justice

Have the class work in groups of three to five students to complete the critical thinking exercise, "Examining Issues of Justice," on p. 172 of the student text. With the class read the directions for completing the exercise and review the questions in the "What do you think?" section before groups begin their work. Have the groups share their responses with the class.

C. Reading and Discussion
Why divide issues of justice into three categories?

Post the three categories of justice on the board:

- **distributive justice**
- **corrective justice**
- **procedural justice**

Ask students to read "Why divide issues of justice into three categories?" on pp. 173-174 of the text. Have the students define each of the categories of justice. Record their responses on the board. Ask students to offer examples for each category either from the reading or from their experience.

Direct attention to the illustrations on p. 173 of the text. Ask students to respond to the questions in the captions:

- How might the division of household chores raise an issue of distributive justice?
- How might responses to cheating on a test raise issues of corrective justice?
- How might the way trials are conducted raise an issue of procedural justice?

To conclude the discussion, direct attention to "Defining Types of Issues" on p. 173. Focus the discussion on question number 2, "Why should we divide issues of justice this way?"

D. Critical Thinking Exercise
Identifying Types of Issues of Justice

Have the class work in small groups or with a study partner to complete the critical thinking exercise, "Identifying Types of Issues of Justice," on pp. 174-175 of the student text. Read the directions for completing the exercise with the class and review the questions in the "What do you think?" section on p. 175.

Students might offer the following responses:

- distributive justice–situations 1 - 4
- corrective justice–situations 5 - 8
- procedural justice–situations 9 - 12

1. **What is fair or unfair about each situation?**
   Encourage students to explain what they think is fair or unfair about each of the situations. Encourage the expression, examination, and evaluation of various positions in each situation.

2. **What similar situations have you experienced or observed?**
   This question should focus students' attention on the relevance of the subject and of the three categories of justice to their daily lives. Encourage students to relate at least one situation they described to the issues raised by each of the examples in the exercise.

E. Concluding the Lesson

Have the class work in groups of three to five students. Distribute newspapers and newsmagazines to each group. Ask students to find articles that involve issues of justice. Have the groups share their articles with the class. Ask them to identify the category or categories of justice the articles describe. To conclude the discussion, ask the class why it might be useful to categorize issues of justice into distributive, corrective, or procedural justice. You may want to have students use the articles to initiate a bulletin board on the topic of justice.

Have students re-read "Purpose of Lesson" on p. 172 of the text. Ask them to describe the extent to which they achieved the objectives of the lesson.

Using the Lesson

The activities suggested in "Using the Lesson" on p. 175 of the text reinforce or extend what students have learned about categorizing issues of justice as distributive, corrective, or procedural justice. When working on any of the activities encourage students to do the following:

- identify the category of justice involved
- think about what might be fair or unfair about the situation
- identify similar situations they might have experienced or observed

Students can work on the three activities suggested in "Using the Lesson" individually or in small groups. Have the students share their work with the class.

This lesson concludes the study of Unit One, "What Is Justice?" If students are keeping a journal, ask them to review the list of things they expected to learn from this unit. Next, ask students to write a summary in their journals of what they have learned about the three categories of justice.

Unit Two: What Is Distributive Justice?

Introduce **Unit Two: What Is Distributive Justice?** Explain to students that Unit Two deals with the subject of distributive justice: the fair distribution of benefits and/or burdens among two or more people or groups in society. Explain that during the first lessons in the unit the class will learn a set of intellectual tools that can be useful in analyzing, taking, and defending a position on issues of distributive justice. The intellectual tools for distributive justice include the following:

- the principle of similarity
- a set of considerations (need, capacity, and desert or deserving) necessary for the use and application of the principle of similarity
- an examination of values and interests useful to consider before taking a position or acting on an issue of distributive justice

In subsequent lessons, students practice using the intellectual tools to deal with issues that involve the distribution of employment and educational opportunities.

Post the following terms on the board:

- **distributive justice**
- **benefits**
- **burdens**

Have the class read "Purpose of Unit" on p. 176 of the student text. Ask students to define **distributive justice**. Record their responses on the board. Their definition should approximate that in the text: how fairly benefits or burdens are distributed among persons or groups in society. Ask students to define **benefits** and to offer examples from the reading or their experience of benefits that might be distributed among persons or groups in society. Ask the students to define **burdens** and to offer examples of burdens that might be distributed among persons or groups in society.

Direct attention to the illustration on p. 176 of the text. Ask students to respond to the question in the caption, "What issues of distributive justice do these pictures illustrate?" Ask students the reason they think some of the most difficult problems we face in our daily lives might concern distributive justice.

Ask students to list three things they expect to learn from their study of Unit Two.

Lesson 2: What Intellectual Tools Are Useful in Examining Issues of Distributive Justice?

Lesson Overview

This lesson focuses students' attention on the **intellectual tools** that can be useful in examining issues of distributive justice. First students learn the **principle of similarity**: in a particular situation, people who are similar in certain ways should be treated alike; people who are different in certain ways should be treated differently. Then students learn to examine similarities and differences among people using the considerations of **need, capacity, and desert**. Finally, students identify the way the principle of similarity and need, capacity, and desert can be used to distribute benefits and burdens in the situations described in the critical thinking exercise.

Lesson Objectives

At the conclusion of this lesson, students should be able to do the following:

- define the principle of similarity
- apply the principle of similarity, using the considerations of need, capacity, and desert, to analyze particular situations
- explain the usefulness of the principle of similarity and considerations of need, capacity, and desert in analyzing issues of distributive justice

Preparation/Materials Required

Student text pp. 177-179

Teaching Procedures

A. Introducing the Lesson

Direct attention to the illustration on p. 177 of the text. Ask students to respond to the question in the caption,

"Why is need important in deciding how medicine should be distributed?" Lead the class to think of important ways in which the people in the illustration are similar. Lead them to think of important ways in which they are different.

While you post the "Terms to Know" on the board, have students read "Purpose of Lesson" on p. 177 of the text.

B. Reading and Discussion
What is the principle of similarity?

Have the class read "What is the principle of similarity?" on pp. 177-178 of the text. Ask students to define the principle of similarity in their own words and to offer an example from the reading or their experience.

C. Reading and Discussion
How are the ideas of need, capacity, and desert used with the principle of similarity?

Post the terms **need, capacity,** and **desert** on the board. Have the class read "How are the ideas of need, capacity, and desert used with the principle of similarity?" on p. 178 of the text. Ask students to briefly define the terms. Remind the class that they will examine the meaning of these terms in more detail in the next lesson.

D. Critical Thinking Exercise
Identifying and Evaluating the Use of the Principle of Similarity

Have the students work with a study partner to complete the critical thinking exercise, "Identifying and Evaluating the Use of the Principle of Similarity," on pp. 178-179 of the student text. With the class read the directions for completing the exercise and review the questions in "Identifying Uses of the Principle of Similarity" on p. 179 of the text. Have the students share their responses with the class. Some responses students might offer are listed on the "Distributive Justice Study Chart" on the next page.

Distributive Justice Study Chart

What benefit or burden was being distributed in each of the situations?	In what important ways were the people or groups similar?	In what important ways were the people or groups different?	Which consideration(s) was used to determine who received the benefit or burden: need, capacity, or desert?
1. opportunity to study at the Academy of Musical Arts	we can infer that all the applicants wanted to study music	some applicants possessed less musical talent or ability than others	those with the least capacity had the greatest need to learn music
2. food	we can infer that all people living on the island needed food for survival	some people on the island were taller than others	shorter people had stomachs with a smaller capacity to hold food; shorter people needed less food
3. child care	we can infer that the residents of Carson City wanted child care at the taxpayers' expense	some residents did not work; some who worked could not afford the cost of child care; some earned more money and could afford to pay for child care	those who did not work did not need child care; those who could not afford child care needed government assistance
4. lakeside houses	we can infer that many people wanted to live in a planned community located next to a lake and that they could afford to do so	some people were excellent swimmers, owned boats, and had received outstanding citizen awards from the city council	people who were excellent swimmers and who owned boats possessed a greater capacity to use the lake; since they were outstanding citizens, too, they were deserving of the privilege
5. right to vote	we can infer that people of all ages wanted to exercise the right to vote	some people were eighteen years old or younger	older people were set in their ways and did not possess the capacity to vote for progress
6. jobs	we can infer that all applicants at the employment agency needed jobs	some people had more children than others; some people possessed greater ability to perform the work than others	people with the most children had a greater need for the jobs even though they might have possessed less capacity to perform the work
7. medical treatment	we can infer that all the people who went to the clinic needed medical care	some people arrived at the clinic earlier than others; some people were more seriously ill than others	people who arrived first were considered more deserving of medical treatment than people who had a greater need

Ask students whether they agree or disagree with the distribution of benefits and burdens in each situation. Encourage students to support their opinions with reasons. Instruct students to save their written responses to the questions in this exercise to use again in Lesson 3.

E. Concluding the Lesson

To conclude the discussion of the principle of similarity, direct attention to the photograph on p. 178 of the text. Ask students to respond to the question in the caption, "Why might government pay the costs of child care only for working parents who could not afford it themselves?"

Have students re-read "Purpose of Lesson" on p. 177 of the text. Ask them to describe the extent to which they achieved the objectives of the lesson.

Using the Lesson

The activities suggested in "Using the Lesson" on p. 179 of the text reinforce or extend what students have learned about the intellectual tools for distributive justice. The activities give students practice in applying the principle of similarity to an issue of distributive justice. When working on any of the activities suggested, encourage students to do the following:

- apply the principle of similarity
- apply the considerations of need, capacity, and desert

You may have students work on these activities individually or in small groups.

Lesson 3: How Can Intellectual Tools Be Used in Examining Issues of Distributive Justice?

Teaching Procedures

A. Introducing the Lesson

Assemble a group of three students at the front of the class. Ask them how they might decide to share something to eat such as a candy bar. After a brief discussion, identify one student as having fasted all day, one as being on a diet, and one as deserving a reward for good performance on a test. Given this additional information, how might they decide to share the item? Explain that in this lesson the class will learn to apply considerations useful in distributing benefits and burdens.

While you post the "Terms to Know" on the board, have students read "Purpose of Lesson" on p. 180 of the text.

B. Reading and Discussion
Using the Principle of Similarity

Have the class read "Using the Principle of Similarity" on p. 180 of the student text. Review the principle of similarity with the class. Ask students to review their responses to the questions in the critical thinking exercise on pp. 178-179 in Lesson 2, "Identifying and Evaluating the Use of the Principle of Similarity." In which situations did they think the distribution of benefits and burdens might have been unfair? Which decisions were based on irrelevant similarities and differences? Remind students that when used properly, the principle of similarity and the ideas of need, capacity, and desert form a set of intellectual tools that can be useful in dealing with issues of distributive justice.

C. Critical Thinking Exercise
Examining Need, Capacity, and Desert

Have students work alone or with a study partner to complete the critical thinking exercise, "Examining Need, Capacity, and Desert," on pp. 180-182 of the text. With the class read the directions for completing the exercise. You may find it useful to review the structure of this exercise with the class. First students read a brief explanation of a consideration, e.g., need. Then they examine an example of need and decide the way to respond to the situation by applying the idea of need. The identical structure is used to examine capacity and desert.

After students complete their responses to the application questions, ask them to share their responses with the class.

Next, review the "What do you think?" questions on p. 182 and ask students to write their responses. Have them share their responses with the class.

D. Reading and Discussion
Taking Other Values and Interests into Account

Have the class read "Taking Other Values and Interests into Account" on p. 182 of the text. Ask students to define the terms **values** and **interests** and to offer examples from the reading or their experience. Record their responses on the board.

E. Critical Thinking Exercise
Weighing Justice Against Conflicting Values and Interests

Have the class work in groups of three to five students to complete the critical thinking exercise, "Weighing Justice Against Conflicting Values and Interests," on pp. 182-183 of the text. The reading selection, "A Disastrous Flood," describes a desert community that needed assistance when a flood devastated it. The community failed to prepare itself for this natural disaster because such events rarely occur in the desert. Read the directions for completing the exercise with the class and review the questions in the "What do you think?" section on p. 183 of the text.

Have the students share their responses with the class. Students should feel free to take any position on this issue that they believe is supported by sound reasoning and a clear explanation of values. The purpose of the exercise is to lead students to understand that in some instances values and interests other than justice may be important in developing a proper position. A strict interpretation of distributive justice in this situation might call for a refusal to provide assistance based on need due to the community's demonstrated lack of responsibility and, therefore, lack of desert. However, a position could be taken that in this situation justice should be tempered with mercy and forgiveness; therefore, assistance should be provided.

F. Critical Thinking Exercise
Examining Common Difficulties in Applying the Principle of Similarity

Have the class work in groups of three to five students to complete the critical thinking exercise, "Examining Common Difficulties in Applying the Principle of Similarity," on p. 183 of the text. With the class read the directions for completing the exercise and review the questions in the "What do you think?" section on p. 184. Remind students that the two most common difficulties in using the principle of similarity are the following:

- disagreement about which similarities or differences among people should be considered in a particular situation
- disagreement about what degree of similarity or difference justifies treating people alike or differently.

Ask students to share their responses with the class.

G. Concluding the Lesson

Direct attention to the illustrations on pp. 180 and 181 of the text. Ask students to respond to the questions in the captions:

- How is the idea of need useful in making fair decisions?
- How is the idea of capacity useful in making fair decisions?
- How is the idea of desert useful in making fair decisions?

Direct attention to the photograph on p. 182 of the text. Ask students to respond to the question in the caption, "Why might it be important to consider other values and interests as well as fairness in making decisions?"

Have students re-read "Purpose of Lesson" on p. 180 of the text. Ask them to describe the extent to which they achieved the objectives of the lesson.

Using the Lesson

The activities suggested in "Using the Lesson" on p. 184 of the text reinforce or extend what students have learned about the intellectual tools for distributive justice. The activities give students practice in applying the principle of similarity and the considerations of need, capacity, and desert to specific situations. When working on any of the activities encourage students to do the following:

- apply the principle of similarity
- apply the considerations of need, capacity, and desert
- consider other values and interests in developing a position on an issue of distributive justice

You may have students work on these activities individually or in small groups.

Lesson 4: Who Should Get the Job?

<table>
<tr><td>

Lesson Overview

Students apply the whole set of intellectual tools to a problem of distributive justice. They read a selection in which a newly elected mayor must fill an important position in city government. Students read brief profiles of four applicants for the position and apply the intellectual tools to develop a position on this issue of distributive justice. Finally, they role-play interviews with the mayor's employment panel during which they present arguments supporting the selection of one of the candidates.

Lesson Objectives

At the conclusion of this lesson, students should be able to do the following:

- use the intellectual tools to develop and support positions on which applicant should be chosen to fill a position in city government
- explain the values and interests that underlie their positions
- evaluate various positions in terms of distributive justice and other values and interests

Preparation/Materials Required

Student text pp. 185-188

A copy for each student of the "Intellectual Tool Chart for Issues of Distributive Justice" on p. 188 of the student text

Optional: Invite an elected official to participate in the lesson with the class

</td></tr>
</table>

Teaching Procedures

A. Introducing the Lesson

Introduce the lesson by asking students how they might use the intellectual tools to decide whom to hire for a position in city government.

B. Critical Thinking Exercise
Selecting Someone for a Position

This critical thinking exercise involves the class in a role-play activity. Before introducing the role-play, post the following roles on the board:

- mayor's employment panel
- Bill Spangler
- Kim Villas
- Charles Daly
- Dotty Vickers

With the class read the directions for participating in the critical thinking exercise, "Selecting Someone for a Position," on p. 185 of the text. Check for student understanding of the duties of the mayor's employment panel and the manner in which the role-play is to be conducted.

Have the class read "Who Should Be Selected as Special Advisor?" on p. 186 of the text. The selection lists the duties of the Special Advisor on Community Relations and describes recommendations to the mayor from her campaign manager and the president of a minority rights group. Ask students to identify the duties of the position; record their responses on the board. Ask students to identify the recommendations of the campaign manager and of the president of the minority rights groups; record their responses on the board. Ask them to identify the values and interests that each recommendation promoted.

Have the class read the portraits of the four candidates for the position of Special Advisor on Community Relations. Ask students to describe each of the candidates.

Divide the class into five groups representing the roles posted on the board. Distribute a copy to each student of the "Intellectual Tool Chart for Issues of Distributive Justice" on p. 188 of the student text. Allow adequate time for the groups to complete the chart and to develop their positions on the issue. For more detailed instructions on conducting a committee hearing refer to p. 12 of this guide.

C. Concluding the Lesson

At the conclusion of the role-play, have the mayor's employment panel share their recommendation with the class on who the mayor should appoint to the

Special Advisor on Community Relations position. Ask the members of the panel to offer reasoning that supports their decision. Record their responses on the board. Ask the class to answer the following:

- What kinds of similarities and differences among the candidates did the panel emphasize in reaching their recommendation?
- What relative weight did they seem to give to the considerations of need, capacity, and desert?
- What were the advantages and disadvantages of doing what is fair in this situation?
- What values and interests other than justice might be served by the panel's recommendation?
- In what way were the intellectual tools for distributive justice helpful in developing and taking a stand on this issue?

Have students re-read "Purpose of Lesson" on p. 185 of the text. Ask them to describe the extent to which they achieved the objectives of the lesson.

Using the Lesson

The activities suggested in "Using the Lesson" on p. 187 of the text reinforce or extend what students have learned about using the intellectual tools for distributive justice. You may have students work on these activities individually or in small groups. Activity number 1 can be used as a journal-writing exercise.

Optional Reinforcement and Enrichment Exercises

You may want to invite an elected official to the class to assist the groups in preparing their presentations. The community resource person might be asked to work with the mayor's employment panel and to participate with the class during the presentation phase of the activity. Be sure that the resource person is familiar with the intellectual tools for distributive justice.

The resource person may also participate in the concluding discussion to help students evaluate the recommendation of the mayor's employment panel and the process used for developing the recommendation. For more information on how to use a community resource person in classroom instruction, refer to p. 11 of this guide.

Lesson 5: How Would You Select Students to Participate in a Music Program?

<table>
<tr><td>

Lesson Overview

Students are provided with a final exercise in applying the intellectual tools for developing and taking a position on an issue of distributive justice. The reading selection describes a school district that lacks the financial resources to provide music instruction for all of its students. When the district receives special funding from the state, the superintendent develops a plan for offering music classes to a limited number of students. This exercise involves the class in evaluating the fairness of the plan and in role-playing a public hearing before the school board.

Lesson Objectives

At the conclusion of this lesson, students should be able to do the following:

- develop and support positions on the fairness of a plan to offer music instruction to a limited number of students
- develop and support positions on proposed modifications or recommend substitute plans

Preparation/Materials Required

Student text pp. 189-192

A copy for each student of the "Intellectual Tool Chart for Issues of Distributive Justice" on p. 192 of the student text

Optional: Invite a member of your school board to participate in the lesson with the class

</td></tr>
</table>

Teaching Procedures

A. Introducing the Lesson

Direct attention to the illustration on p. 189 of the student text. Ask students to respond to the question in the caption, "What do you think would be a fair way to select students for music education classes?"

B. Critical Thinking Exercise
Evaluating the Fairness of a Plan

In the two critical thinking exercises in this lesson, the class role-plays a public hearing before a school board. This segment of the lesson develops the background information for participating in the activity.

Have the class read the critical thinking exercise, "Evaluating the Fairness of a Plan," on pp. 189-190 of the student text. The reading selection, "The Music Program," describes a plan developed by the superintendent of schools for providing music instruction to a limited number of students in the district. Ask students to describe the circumstances leading to the proposed plan and the details of the plan itself. Record their responses on the board.

C. Critical Thinking Exercise
Role-Playing a School Board Hearing

Before introducing the role-play, post the following four roles on the board:

- School Superintendent and staff
- Students and Parents for Equality
- Music Appreciation Society
- Farmington School Board

Have the class read the critical thinking exercise, "Role-Playing a School Board Hearing," on pp. 190-91 of the text. Ask students to describe each of the roles represented in the activity. Review the directions for conducting the school board hearing with the class. Divide the class into four groups representing the roles posted on the board. Allow adequate time for groups to evaluate the proposed plan and to prepare their positions or alternate plans on this issue of distributive justice. Distribute a copy to each student of the "Intellectual Tool Chart for Issues of Distributive Justice" on p. 192 of the student text.

If you have invited a school board member to the class ask him or her to join the students assigned to play the role of the Farmington School Board. This community resource person can assist the students in preparing their role as well as participating in the hearing itself. It is important that the resource person remain with the class during the concluding portion of the lesson to help evaluate the proposals and to share with the class the way your school board makes policy decisions involving issues of distributive justice.

For more detailed instructions on conducting a public hearing refer to p. 12 of this guide.

D. Concluding the Lesson

At the conclusion of the role-play, have the Farmington School Board share their decision with the class on the way they will distribute opportunities to participate in the music education program. Ask the members of the Board to explain their reasoning supporting the decision. Record their responses on the board. Encourage the school board member whom you have invited to the class to participate in the discussion that follows. Ask the class to answer the following:

- What kinds of similarities and differences among the potential music students did the board emphasize in reaching their decision?

- What relative weight did they seem to give to the considerations of need, capacity, and desert?

- What were the advantages and disadvantages of doing what is fair in this situation?

- What values and interests other than justice might be served by the board's decision?

- In what way were the intellectual tools for distributive justice helpful in developing and taking a stand on this issue?

Conclude the discussion by asking your community resource person to share the way your school board makes policy decisions involving issues of distributive justice with the class.

Have students re-read "Purpose of Lesson" on p. 189 of the text. Ask them to describe the extent to which they achieved the objectives of the lesson.

Using the Lesson

The activities suggested in "Using the Lesson" on p. 191 of the text reinforce or extend what students have learned about using the intellectual tools for distributive justice. You may have students work on these activities individually or in small groups.

This lesson concludes the study of Unit Two, "What Is Distributive Justice?" If students are keeping a journal, ask them to review the list of things they expected to learn in this unit. Ask students to write a summary in their journals of what they have learned about using intellectual tools to develop and take positions on issues of distributive justice.

Teacher References

Activity number 3 in "Using the Lesson" on p. 191 of the text suggests that students read the United States Supreme Court decision in *Fullilove v. Klutznick*, 448 U.S. 448 (1980). The case challenged the constitutionality of the 1977 Public Works Employment Act. The law requires that at least ten percent of federal funds granted for local public works projects be used to purchase services and supplies from minority businesses. State and local governments may waive certain important requirements, such as bonding and lowest bid, to comply with the law.

Several non-minority contractors filed suit, claiming that they suffered economic loss as a result of this law. However, the Supreme Court disagreed. The Court said that the Public Works Employment Act is within the power of Congress to enforce equal protection guarantees in the Fourteenth Amendment. The Court rejected the idea that Congress must act in a wholly "color blind" fashion when trying to remedy the effects of past discrimination. Where federal anti-discrimination laws have been violated, an equitable remedy may include a racial or ethnic factor.

The three dissenting justices were not persuaded. They wrote that government endorsement of racial classifications perpetuates the socially divisive belief that race should count.

Unit Three: What Is Corrective Justice?

Introduce **Unit Three: What Is Corrective Justice?** Direct attention to the illustration on p. 193 of the student text.

Ask students to identify the situations shown in the illustration. Record their responses on the board. On the basis of the situations identified, ask students to predict the definition of corrective justice. Ask the class to respond to the question in the caption, "How do the situations illustrated in these pictures raise issues of corrective justice"?

Explain that in this unit the class will learn about fair and proper responses to wrongs and injuries. During the early lessons in the unit, students learn about the need for and principal goals of corrective justice. Then they learn a set of intellectual tools for evaluating, taking, and defending responses to wrongs and injuries. The intellectual tools include the following five basic steps.

1. Identify wrongs and injuries.

2. Identify important characteristics of persons or groups causing wrongs or injuries.

3. Identify important characteristics of persons or groups wronged or injured.

4. Examine alternative responses to wrongs and injuries and their purposes.

5. Consider related values and interests.

Finally, in subsequent lessons students use the intellectual tools to deal with two issues of corrective justice. One issue involves fraud and theft resulting from a broken contract and the other involves environmental pollution.

Have the class read "Purpose of Unit" on p. 193 of the student text. Ask students to list four things they expect to learn from their study of Unit Three.

Lesson 6: What Are the Goals of Corrective Justice?

Lesson Overview

Students learn that corrective justice means fair and proper responses to wrongs or injuries. Through class discussion of three brief selections raising issues of corrective justice, students learn about the need for corrective justice in society. They learn that the goals of corrective justice are to **correct**, **prevent**, and **deter** wrongs and injuries.

Lesson Objectives

At the conclusion of this lesson, students should be able to do the following:

- define corrective justice
- explain the goals of corrective justice
- identify situations involving wrongs and injuries

Preparation/Materials Required

Student text pp. 194-195

A copy for each student of a newspaper article that describes a response to a wrong, injury, or both

---

Teaching Procedures

A. Introducing the Lesson

To each student distribute a copy of a newspaper article that describes a response to a wrong, injury, or both. Have the class read the article and discuss whether or not students think the response is fair and proper.

While you post "Terms to Know" on the board, have students read "Purpose of Lesson" on p. 194 of the text.

B. Critical Thinking Exercise

Examining Issues of Corrective Justice

Have the class work in groups of three to five students to complete the critical thinking exercise, "Examining Issues of Corrective Justice," on p. 194 of the student text. Read the directions for completing the exercise with the class and review the questions in the "What do you think?" section on pp. 194-195. Have the students share their responses with the class.

C. Reading and Discussion

What is the need for corrective justice?

Post the term **corrective justice** on the board. Have the class read "What is the need for corrective justice?" on p. 195 of the text. Ask students to define the term posted on the board. Discuss why they think that people living together in groups creates a need for corrective justice. Ask students to use their own experiences to identify situations where corrective justice might have been needed. Record their responses on the board. Ask students to identify some of the common responses to wrongs or injuries discussed in the text. Discuss the way these responses might help correct the situations that the students described.

D. Reading and Discussion

What are the goals of corrective justice?

Have the class read "What are the goals of corrective justice?" on p. 195 of the text. Help students understand that the basic goal of corrective justice is to "set things right" in a fair way when a wrong or injury has occurred. With the class discuss the reason that they think it might be important to set things right in a fair way. Explain that there are additional goals of corrective justice. Ask students to define the following terms: **correction**, **prevention**, and **deterrence**. Discuss why the class thinks these additional goals might be important to society.

E. Concluding the Lesson

Ask students to identify a person they know or have read about who had to deal with a situation involving an issue of corrective justice. The range of potential people includes judges, teachers, principals, parents, students, etc. Have students draw a cartoon illustrating the way that person dealt with the situation. Ask students to write a caption for their drawing that explains which goal(s) of corrective justice (correction, prevention, deterrence) the person was trying to achieve in the way he or she dealt with the situation. Have students share their work with the class.

Have students re-read "Purpose of Lesson" on p. 194 of the text. Ask them to describe the extent to which they achieved the objectives of the lesson.

Lesson 7: What Intellectual Tools Are Useful in Making Decisions About Issues of Corrective Justice?

Lesson Overview

Students are introduced to the first three of the five steps of the intellectual tools useful in dealing with issues of corrective justice. The first three steps focus on identifying these important characteristics: 1. wrongs and injuries; 2. persons or groups causing the wrong or injury; and 3. persons or groups wronged or injured. Students learn key terms and apply the three steps to situations described in the text.

Lesson Objectives

At the conclusion of this lesson, students should be able to do the following:

■ define the terms used in the intellectual tools for corrective justice

■ explain and use the first three steps of the intellectual tools used in dealing with issues of corrective justice

Preparation/Materials Required

Student text pp. 196-200

Newspapers and/or newsmagazines for each group of three students

Optional: A copy for each student of the "Intellectual Tool Chart for Issues of Corrective Justice" on p. 209 of the student text (steps 1-3 only)

Teaching Procedures

A. Introducing the Lesson

Remind the class of the usefulness of using intellectual tools in evaluating, taking, and defending positions on different issues of justice.

While you post "Terms to Know" on the board, have students read "Purpose of Lesson" on p. 196 of the text.

B. Reading and Discussion
How can we decide upon fair or proper responses to wrongs and injuries?

Have the class read "How can we decide upon fair or proper responses to wrongs and injuries?" on p. 196 of the student text. Remind students that the basic goal of corrective justice is to set things right in a fair way when a wrong or injury has happened. Discuss why students think deciding what is fair might be simple in some situations and more complicated in others. Ask students to cite examples from their reading. Remind the class that intellectual tools can be helpful in deciding what to do in such situations.

C. Critical Thinking Exercise
Examining Intellectual Tools

This critical thinking exercise introduces the first three of five steps of the intellectual tools for corrective justice. Students will learn the other two steps in Lesson 8. Post the three steps on the board:

1. **Identify the important characteristics of the wrong or injury.**

2. **Identify the important characteristics of the person or persons causing the wrong or injury.**
3. **Identify the important characteristics of the person or persons who were wronged or injured.**

As you discuss the material in this lesson, record relevant terms and information associated with each step on the board. The emphasis should be on comprehension of the tools, their application to the situations presented, and their application to situations students may have experienced or observed.

Have the students read the critical thinking exercise, "Examining Intellectual Tools," on pp. 196-200 of the text. This exercise may best be accomplished through reading and directed class discussion. However, you may want the class to work in small groups. If so, assign a portion of the text to each group and ask them to present the material to the class.

Discuss Step 1. Ask students to read section 1-a. Ask them to define the terms **wrong** and **injury**. Record their responses on the board. Remind students that in some cases conduct may be wrong and also cause an injury. Ask students to examine the examples in 1-a and classify them as wrongs, injuries, or both.

Discuss section 1-b with the class. Remind students that when dealing with issues of corrective justice we also want to know the seriousness of the wrong or injury, including the following:

(1) **extent**
(2) **duration**
(3) **impact**
(4) **offensiveness**

Define terms where necessary and examine the examples cited in the text.

Discuss Step 2. Ask students to read section 2-a. Ask them what is meant by a person's **state of mind**. Remind the class that to determine a person's state of mind, one should consider the following:

(1) **intent**
(2) **recklessness**
(3) **carelessness**
(4) **knowledge of probable consequences**
(5) **control**
(6) **duty or obligation**
(7) **more important values and interests**

Have the students read a-(1) through a-(7). Define terms where necessary and examine the examples cited in the material.

Have the students read the imaginary situation describing the accusations against Xavier Kahn, the commander of an imaginary space ship. Using questions a-(1) through a-(7), ask students to analyze Xavier Kahn's state of mind during the events described. Ask them to share their responses with the class. Discuss steps 2-b through 2-e with the class:

b. **past history**
c. **character**
d. **feelings**
e. **person's role** in causing the wrong or injury

Define terms where necessary and examine the examples cited in the text.

Discuss Step 3. Explain that it is also important to know characteristics of the person or persons who suffered the wrong or injury. Have the class read 3-a and 3-b. Define terms where necessary and examine the examples cited in the text.

Have the class respond to the questions in the "What do you think?" section on p. 200. Ask students to share their responses with the class.

D. Concluding the Lesson

Have the class work in groups of three to five students. Distribute newspapers and newsmagazines to each group. Ask students to locate articles on issues of corrective justice. Have students determine which of the intellectual tools were used in making decisions about responding to the wrongs and injuries described in the articles. Ask students to share their work with the class.

Have students re-read "Purpose of Lesson" on p. 196 of the text. Ask them to describe the extent to which they achieved the objectives of the lesson.

Using the Lesson

The activities suggested in "Using the Lesson" on p. 200 of the text reinforce or extend what students have learned about intellectual tools used in dealing with issues of corrective justice. When working on the activities suggested, encourage students to use the three steps. Students may work on the activities individually or in small groups.

Lesson 8: What Responses Can We Make to Wrongs and Injuries?

Lesson Overview

This lesson introduces students to the remaining two steps of the intellectual tools useful in dealing with issues of corrective justice:

4. examining alternative responses to wrongs and injuries and their purposes,

5. considering related values and interests.

Students learn key terms and apply the two steps to situations described in the text. Then students apply all five steps of the intellectual tools to deal with a situation involving an automobile accident caused by a person driving under the influence of alcohol.

Lesson Objectives

At the conclusion of this lesson, students should be able to do the following:

- define the terms used in the intellectual tools for corrective justice

- explain various responses that might be useful in dealing with wrongs and injuries, the purposes of each type of response, and their usefulness in achieving the goals of correction, deterrence, or prevention

- use the five steps of the intellectual tools to evaluate, take, and defend a position in a situation involving an issue of corrective justice

Preparation/Materials Required

Student text pp. 201-210

A copy for each student of the "Intellectual Tool Chart for Issues of Corrective Justice" on pp. 209-210 of the student text

Teaching Procedures

A. Introducing the Lesson

While you post "Terms to Know" on the board, have students read "Purpose of Lesson" on p. 201 of the text.

B. Reading and Discussion
What are the five steps to use in examining issues of corrective justice?

This material gives an overview of the five steps of the intellectual tools for corrective justice. Have the class read "What are the five steps to use in examining issues of corrective justice?" on p. 201 of the student text. Review the first three steps studied in Lesson 7. Post the remaining two steps on the board:

4. **Examine common responses to wrongs and injuries and their purposes.**

5. **Consider other values and interests in determining a response.**

C. Critical Thinking Exercise
Examining Intellectual Tools

During this critical thinking exercise students examine the remaining two steps of the intellectual tools for corrective justice. As you discuss the material in this lesson, record relevant terms and information associated with each step on the board.

Have the students read the critical thinking exercise, "Examining Intellectual Tools," on pp. 201-207 of the text. This exercise may best be accomplished through reading and directed class discussion. You may, however, want the class to work in small groups. If so, assign a portion of the text to each group and ask them to present the material to the class.

Discuss Step 4. Remind students that the goals of corrective justice are correction, prevention, and deterrence. Explain that a number of responses to wrongs and injuries might be made to achieve these goals, including the following:

a. **to inform**

b. **to overlook** or **to ignore**

c. **to forgive** or **to pardon**

d. **to punish**
e. **to restore**
f. **to compensate**
g. **to provide treatment or education**

Ask students to read sections 4-a through 4-g. Discuss each section with the class. Define terms where necessary and examine the examples cited in the text. Discuss the purpose or goals each response to a wrong or injury can achieve.

Discuss Step 5. Explain to the class that when we try to decide what response to make to a wrong or injury, we need to consider related values and interests that may be promoted or undermined by a particular response. The values or interests we should consider include the following:

a. **correction** of the wrong or injury
b. **deterrence** or **prevention** of future wrongs or injuries
c. **distributive justice**
d. **human dignity**
e. **preservation of human life**
f. **practicality**
g. **freedom**
h. **proportionality**
i. **revenge**

Ask students to read sections 5-a through 5-i. Discuss each section with the class. Define terms where necessary and examine the examples cited in the text. Explain that sometimes there may be a conflict between the values and the interests they have studied. Read the examples on p. 207 and encourage students to offer additional examples.

Have the class respond to the questions in the "What do you think?" section on p. 207. Ask students to share their responses with the class.

D. Critical Thinking Exercise
Taking Positions on an Issue of Corrective Justice

Have the class work in groups of three to five students to complete the critical thinking exercise, "Taking Positions on an Issue of Corrective Justice," on pp. 207-208 of the text. The reading selection, "The Accident," describes a situation in which a person who was driving while intoxicated is responsible for the damages suffered by another motorist. With the class read the directions for completing the exercise and review the questions in the "What do you think?" section on p. 208. Distribute a copy to each student of the "Intellectual Tool Chart for Issues of Corrective Justice" on pp. 209-210 of the student text. Allow adequate time for students to apply the five steps to evaluate, take, and defend a response to the wrongs and injuries described in the reading selection.

E. Concluding the Lesson

Ask students to share their responses with the class using the intellectual tools to evaluate, take, and defend a position in response to the wrongs and injuries described in the critical thinking exercise. You may want students to actually "take a stand" by asking them to respond to the statement: Drunk drivers habituated to alcohol should be helped with medical treatment rather than punished through the criminal justice system. Post five signs around the classroom (strongly agree, agree, undecided, disagree, and strongly disagree). Ask students to stand by the words that most closely reflect their thinking on this issue. Allow time for students to share their reasoning. For more detailed instructions on conducting this activity refer to p. 24 of this guide.

Have students re-read "Purpose of Lesson" on p. 196 of the text. Ask them to describe the extent to which they achieved the objectives of the lesson.

Using the Lesson

The activities suggested in "Using the Lesson" on p. 208 of the text reinforce or extend what students have learned about intellectual tools used in dealing with issues of corrective justice. When working on the activities suggested, encourage students to use the five steps they have learned in the lesson. Students may work on the activities individually or in small groups.

Lesson 9: How Would You Respond to the Wrongs and Injuries Described in This Selection?

Lesson Overview

Students are given an opportunity to apply the intellectual tools to evaluate and develop responses to a situation involving **fraud**, a broken contract, and **theft**. The reading selection describes the events that led to wrongs and injuries when two famous rock-and-roll stars changed their minds about a highly promoted concert performance.

Lesson Objectives

At the conclusion of this lesson, students should be able to do the following:

- evaluate a situation involving wrongs and injuries
- take and defend positions on fair and proper responses to the wrongs and injuries using the intellectual tools

Preparation/Materials Required

Student text pp. 211-212

A copy for each student of the "Intellectual Tool Chart for Issues of Corrective Justice" on pp. 209-210 of the student text

Optional: Invite a community resource person such as a judge or attorney to class

Teaching Procedures

A. Introducing the Lesson

While you post the "Terms to Know" on the board, have students read "Purpose of Lesson" on p. 211 of the text.

B. Critical Thinking Exercise
Taking Positions on an Issue of Corrective Justice

Have the class work in groups of three to five students to complete the critical thinking exercise, "Taking Positions on an Issue of Corrective Justice," on pp. 211-212 of the student text. The reading selection describes the wrongs and injuries that occurred when Sly and Freddy, two famous rock-and-roll stars, decided not to give a concert performance in Los Angeles. With the class read the directions for completing the exercise and review the questions in the "What do you think?" section on p. 212. To each student distribute a copy of the "Intellectual Tool Chart for Issues of Corrective Justice" on pp. 209-210 of the student text. Allow adequate time for students to evaluate the wrongs and injuries in this situation and to develop what they believe to be proper responses to the issues. You may want to invite a judge or attorney to the class to help students understand the legal issues in this situation. It is important that the resource person remain with the class during the concluding discussion to help students evaluate the responses to the wrongs and injuries in this situation.

C. Concluding the Lesson

Ask students to share their responses with the class to the wrongs and injuries in this situation. Ask students to answer the following:

- Did the responses fairly and properly correct the wrongs and injuries described in the case?
- How might the responses prevent and deter further wrongs and injuries?
- What other values and interests might have been important to consider in this situation?
- What was the usefulness of using the five-step procedure for deciding what to do in this situation?

Have students re-read "Purpose of Lesson" on p. 211 of the text. Ask them to describe the extent to which they achieved the objectives of the lesson.

Optional Reinforcement and Enrichment Exercises

The reading selection provides an opportunity for role-playing a court hearing to decide fair and proper responses to wrongs and injuries. The activity involves four roles:

- attorney for Sly Mercury and Freddy Steele
- judge
- attorney for Leon Carter
- attorney for Don Richter

You may invite a judge or attorney to class to help students prepare their roles and to participate in the discussion. More instructions for conducting a simulated court hearing are on p. 17 of this guide.

Lesson 10: What Would Be the Proper Responses to the River Pollution Described in This Selection?

Lesson Overview

This lesson provides students with a final exercise in applying the intellectual tools for deciding an issue of corrective justice. The reading selection describes a problem of environmental pollution caused when a corporation failed to install a filtration system to prevent poisonous chemicals from seeping into the river. Students role-play a town council meeting to decide a proper response to the wrongs and injuries in this situation.

Lesson Objectives

At the conclusion of this lesson, students should be able to do the following:

- evaluate a situation involving wrongs and injuries
- take and defend positions on fair and proper responses to the wrongs and injuries using the intellectual tools

Preparation/Materials Required

Student text pp. 213-215

A copy for each student of the "Intellectual Tool Chart for Issues of Corrective Justice" on pp. 209-210 of the student text.

Optional: A community resource person such as a judge or attorney

Teaching Procedures

A. Introducing the Lesson

Ask students to identify some environmental problems in your state or community. Ask them how they might decide to fairly and properly correct the situation.

Have students read "Purpose of Lesson" on p. 213 of the text.

B. Critical Thinking Exercise
Taking Positions on an Environmental Issue

This critical thinking exercise involves role-playing a town council meeting. The reading selection, "James Creek," describes the economic benefits to a small town as the result of a chemical plant locating there. A problem arose, however, when the company failed to install a filter to prevent poisonous chemicals from seeping into the river.

Have the class work in groups of three to five students to complete the critical thinking exercise, "Taking Positions on an Environmental Issue," on pp. 213-215 of the student text. With the class read the directions for completing the exercise and review the questions in the "What do you think?" section on p. 215. To each student distribute a copy of the "Intellectual Tool Chart for Issues of Corrective Justice" on pp. 209-210 of the student text. Allow adequate time for students to evaluate the wrongs and injuries in this situation and to develop what they believe to be proper responses to the issues. You may want to invite a judge or attorney to the class to help students understand the law and legal issues in this situation.

For detailed instructions on conducting a town council meeting refer to p. 21 of this guide.

C. Concluding the Lesson

At the conclusion of the role-play, have the town council share with the class their responses to the wrongs and injuries in this situation. Ask the members of the town council to offer reasoning supporting their decisions. Record their responses on the board. Encourage your community resource person to participate in the discussion that follows. Ask the class to answer the following:

- Did the responses fairly and properly correct the wrongs and injuries in this situation?

- How might the responses prevent and deter further wrongs and injuries?

- What other values and interests did the responses seem to take into consideration?

- In what way were the intellectual tools for corrective justice helpful in evaluating and taking a position on this issue?

Have students re-read "Purpose of Lesson" on p. 213 of the text. Ask them to describe the extent to which they achieved the objectives of the lesson.

Using the Lesson

The activities suggested in "Using the Lesson" on p. 215 of the text reinforce or extend what students have learned about intellectual tools used in dealing with issues of corrective justice. When working on the activities suggested, encourage students to use the five steps they have learned in the lesson. Students may work on the activities individually or in small groups.

This lesson concludes the study of Unit Three, "What Is Corrective Justice?" If students are keeping a journal, have them write a summary in their journals of what they have learned about using intellectual tools to develop and take positions on issues of corrective justice.

Unit Four: What Is Procedural Justice?

Introduce **Unit Four: What Is Procedural Justice?** Direct attention to the illustration on p. 216 of the student text. Ask students to identify the situations in the pictures. Ask them to respond to the question in the caption, "How do the situations illustrated in these pictures show issues of procedural justice?"

Explain that in Unit Four the class will learn about issues of fairness in the ways people gather information and make decisions. They will learn the following goals of procedural justice:

- to increase the chances of discovering information necessary to make wise and just decisions
- to ensure the wise and fair use of the information in making decisions
- to protect important values and interests such as the right to privacy, human dignity, freedom, distributive justice, and efficiency

The first lessons in this unit introduce students to the goals and importance of procedural justice not only in law enforcement and the courts, but also in the executive and legislative branches of government.

Students learn to identify situations involving procedural justice and the four steps of the intellectual tools useful in dealing with those situations. The intellectual tools include the following:

1. Identify the purposes of the information-gathering procedures.

2. Evaluate the procedures used to gather information.

3. Evaluate the procedures used to make a decision.

4. Consider related values and interests.

In subsequent lessons students use the intellectual tools to deal with two issues of procedural justice. One issue involves the ways school administrators gathered information and made decisions regarding cheating on a state examination and the other involves citizens' right to vote.

Have the class read "Purpose of Unit" on p. 216 of the student text. Ask students to list three things they expect to learn from their study of Unit Four.

Lesson 11: What Is Procedural Justice?

Lesson Overview

Students are introduced to the subject of **procedural justice**. Students learn that procedural justice refers to the fairness of the ways people gather information and make decisions. They learn to identify situations involving issues of procedural justice and the reasons procedural justice is important not only in law-enforcement and the courts, but also in the executive and legislative branches of government.

Lesson Objectives

At the conclusion of this lesson, students should be able to do the following:

- define and explain the importance of procedural justice
- identify situations involving issues of procedural justice

Preparation/Materials Required

Student text pp. 217-220

A copy of the **Bill of Rights** for each group of three students

---

Teaching Procedures

A. Introducing the Lesson

Ask students to imagine that they are the subject of a court trial. What might be some of their concerns about the information presented to the court? What procedures would they want the court to follow in trying to determine their guilt or innocence?

While you post the "Terms to Know" on the board, have students read "Purpose of Lesson" on p. 217 of the text.

B. Reading and Discussion
What are the purposes of procedural justice?

Have the class read "What are the purposes of procedural justice?" on p. 217 of the student text. Ask students to define the term **procedural justice**. Ask students to identify three goals that procedural justice is designed to accomplish. Their responses should include the following:

- to increase the chances of discovering information necessary to make wise and just decisions
- to ensure the wise and fair use of the information in making decisions
- to protect important values and interests, such as the right to privacy, human dignity, freedom, distributive justice, and efficiency

C. Critical Thinking Exercise
Examining Issues of Procedural Justice

Have students work with a study partner to complete the critical thinking exercise, "Examining Issues of Procedural Justice," on pp. 217-218 of the text. With the class read the directions for completing the exercise and review the questions in the "What do you think?" section on p. 218. Ask students to share their responses with the class.

D. Reading and Discussion
Why is procedural justice important?

Have the class read "Why is procedural justice important?" on p. 218 of the text. Discuss their responses to the questions in the "What do you think?" section on p. 218.

E. Reading and Discussion
Why are law enforcement agencies and the courts responsible for using fair procedures?

Have the class read "Why are law enforcement agencies and the courts responsible for using fair procedures?" on pp. 218-219 of the text. Discuss the way students think procedural justice limits the authority of law enforcement and the courts.

Have the class work in groups of three students. Distribute a copy of the Bill of Rights to each group. Ask students to examine Amendments Four, Five, Six, and Seven and to identify some basic rules for procedural justice the Founders included in the United States Constitution. Ask students the reason they think each rule might be important in ensuring that citizens are treated fairly by their government. What important values and interests do these rules require our government to respect?

F. Reading and Discussion
The Executive and Legislative Branches of Government

Have the class read "The Executive and Legislative Branches of Government" on pp. 219-220 of the text. Discuss their responses to the questions in the "What do you think?" section on p. 220.

G. Concluding the Lesson

Direct attention to the illustrations on pp. 218, 219, and the photograph on p. 220. Ask students to respond to the questions in the captions:

- Why might it be important to require that fair procedures be used to gather information?

- How does the right to trial by jury help guarantee a fair hearing for people accused of crimes?

- What other rights can you think of that help guarantee a fair hearing?

- Why should we be concerned about the procedures used by the executive and legislative branches of government?

Have students re-read "Purpose of Lesson" on p. 217 of the text. Ask them to describe the extent to which they achieved the objectives of the lesson.

Using the Lesson

The activities suggested in "Using the Lesson" on p. 220 of the text reinforce or extend what students have learned about the definition, goals, and importance of procedural justice. When working on any of the activities suggested, encourage students to use the terms they have learned in the lesson. Students may work on the activities individually or in small groups.

Lesson 12: How Can You Evaluate Procedures to Decide If They Are Fair?

Lesson Overview

Students review the goals of procedural justice. Then they are introduced to three of the four steps of the intellectual tools useful in dealing with issues of procedural justice:

1. Identify the purposes of the information-gathering procedures.

2. Evaluate the procedures used to gather information.

3. Evaluate the procedures used to make a decision.

Students learn key terms and apply the three steps to situations described in the text.

Lesson Objectives

At the conclusion of this lesson, students should be able to do the following:

- identify and explain three of the four steps in the intellectual tools used in dealing with issues of procedural justice

- explain the usefulness of the tools in evaluating the fairness of procedures

Preparation/Materials Required

Student text pp. 221-224

Newspapers and/or newsmagazines for each group of three to five students

Optional: A copy for each student of the "Intellectual Tool Chart for Issues of Procedural Justice" on p. 229 of the student text (steps 1-3 only)

Teaching Procedures

A. Introducing the Lesson

Direct attention to the illustrations on pp. 222-224 of the text. Ask students to respond to the questions in the captions:

- What information is sought at public hearings?
- Why is it important to give adequate notice of a hearing?
- Why is it important to make sure people accused of crimes can effectively present the information they wish to have considered?
- Why is the right to a public trial important?

While you post the "Terms to Know" on the board, have students read "Purpose of Lesson" on p. 221 of the text.

B. Reading and Discussion
What ideas are useful in examining issues of procedural justice?

Have the class read "What ideas are useful in examining issues of procedural justice?" on p. 221 of the student text. Review the basic goals of procedural justice with the class and explain that the goals can be used to help us decide whether or not procedures are fair. Explain that the intellectual tools in this lesson will help them evaluate how well the procedures serve the first two goals of procedural justice.

C. Critical Thinking Exercise
Examining Intellectual Tools

This critical thinking exercise introduces three of the four steps of the intellectual tools for procedural justice. Students will learn the fourth step in Lesson 13. Post the three steps on the board:

1. Identify the purposes of the information-gathering procedures.

2. Evaluate the procedures used to gather information.

3. Evaluate the procedures used to make a decision.

As you discuss the material in this lesson, record relevant terms and information associated with each step on the board. The emphasis should be on comprehension of the tools, their application to the situations presented, and their application to situations students may have experienced or observed.

Have the class read the critical thinking exercise, "Examining Intellectual Tools," on pp. 221-224 of the student text. This exercise may best be accomplished through reading and directed class discussion. If you want the class to work in small groups, however, assign a portion of the text to each group and ask them to present the material to the class.

Discuss Step 1. Have the class read Step 1 and ask students to identify the key questions used to **identify the purposes of the information-gathering procedures:**

- **What information is being sought?**
- **Why is this information needed?**

Have the class read the two examples cited and then apply the questions to determine what information is being sought in each situation and why it is needed.

Discuss Step 2. Have the class read Step 2 and ask students to identify the key question used to **evaluate the procedures used to gather information:**

- **Do the procedures ensure that all reliable information necessary for making a wise and just decision is gathered?**

Remind the class that to determine whether or not all reliable information has been gathered, one should consider the following:

(a) **comprehensiveness**

(b) **notice**

(c) **effective presentation**

(d) **predictability** and **flexibility**

(e) **reliability**

Define terms where necessary and examine the examples cited in the material.

Discuss Step 3. Have the class read Step 3 and ask students to identify the key question used to **evaluate the procedures used to make a decision:**

- **Do the procedures ensure that the information gathered will be used wisely and fairly?**

Remind the class that to determine whether or not information is used wisely and fairly, one should consider the following:

(a) **impartiality**

(b) **public observation**

(c) **provision for the detection and correction of errors**

Define terms where necessary and examine the examples cited in the text.

Have the class respond to the questions in the "What do you think?" section on p. 224. Ask students to share their responses with the class.

D. Concluding the Lesson

Have the class work in groups of three to five students. Distribute newspapers and/or newsmagazines to each group. Ask students to locate articles on issues of procedural justice. You may want to distribute a copy to each student of the "Intellectual Tool Chart for Issues of Procedural Justice" on p. 229 of the student text (steps 1-3 only). Ask students to apply the intellectual tools to the articles they have selected. Ask students to share their work with the class.

Have students re-read "Purpose of Lesson" on p. 221 of the text. Ask them to describe the extent to which they achieved the objectives of the lesson.

Using the Lesson

The activities suggested in "Using the Lesson" on p. 224 of the text reinforce or extend what students have learned about intellectual tools used in dealing with issues of procedural justice. When working on the activities, encourage students to use the three steps they learned in the lesson.

Lesson 13: What Other Values and Interests Should Be Considered in Deciding Whether Procedures Are Fair?

Lesson Overview

This lesson provides students with the fourth step of the intellectual tools for dealing with issues of procedural justice:

4. Consider related values and interests.

Students learn that important related values and interests include privacy and freedom, human dignity, distributive justice, and practical considerations. Students then apply the full set of intellectual tools to analyze the procedures used during the trial of Sir Walter Raleigh (1603) on charges of treason against King James I of England.

Lesson Objectives

At the conclusion of this lesson, students should be able to do the following:

- identify and explain the fourth step in the intellectual tools used in dealing with issues of procedural justice
- use the intellectual tools to develop and support positions on an issue of procedural justice

Preparation/Materials Required

Student text pp. 225-229

A copy for each student of the "Intellectual Tool Chart for Issues of Procedural Justice" on p. 229 of the student text

Teaching Procedures

A. Introducing the Lesson

Have students read "Purpose of Lesson" on p. 225 of the text.

B. Reading and Discussion
Considering Related Values and Interests

Have the class read "Considering Related Values and Interests" on p. 225 of the student text. Remind students that while some procedures might be effective for gathering information, they might be unfair because they violate important values and interests such as privacy and human dignity.

C. Critical Thinking Exercise
Examining Intellectual Tools

During this critical thinking exercise students examine the fourth step of the intellectual tools for procedural justice. Post the fourth step on the board:

4. Consider related values and interests.

As you discuss the material in this lesson, record relevant terms and information associated with step four on the board.

Have the class read the critical thinking exercise, "Examining Intellectual Tools," on pp. 225-226 of the student text. This exercise may best be accomplished through reading and directed class discussion. If you want the class to work in small groups, however, assign a portion of the text to each group and ask them to present the material to the class.

Discuss Step 4. Have the class read Step 4 and ask students to identify the key question to **help ensure the protection of other important values and interests:**

- **Do the procedures protect related values and interests?**

Remind the class that to determine whether or not the procedures protect important values and interests, we should consider if the procedures violate the following:

(a) the **right to privacy** or **freedom**

(b) basic ideas of **human dignity**

(c) principles of **distributive justice**

(d) reasonable **practical considerations**

Define terms where necessary and examine the examples cited in the text.

Have the class respond to the questions in the "What do you think?" section on p. 227. Ask students to share their responses with the class.

D. Critical Thinking Exercise
Evaluating Procedures in a Famous Trial

Have the class work in groups of three to five students to complete the critical thinking exercise, "Evaluating Procedures in a Famous Trial," on pp. 227-228 of the text. The reading selection, "The Trial of Sir Walter Raleigh," describes the procedures used to gather information and to decide if the famous explorer was guilty of treason against the King of England. With the class read the directions for completing the exercise and review the questions in the "What do you think?" section on p. 228. Distribute a copy to each student of the "Intellectual Tool Chart for Issues of Procedural Justice" on p. 229 of the student text. Allow adequate time for students to evaluate the procedures and to develop positions on the issues in this situation.

E. Concluding the Lesson

Ask students to share their responses with the class using the intellectual tools to evaluate and to take a position on procedures used to gather information and to make the decision described in the critical thinking exercise.

Have students re-read "Purpose of Lesson" on p. 225 of the text. Ask them to describe the extent to which they achieved the objectives of the lesson.

Using the Lesson

The activities suggested in "Using the Lesson" on p. 228 of the text reinforce or extend what students have learned about intellectual tools used in dealing with issues of procedural justice. When working on the activities suggested, encourage students to address the four steps they learned in Lessons 12 and 13. Students may work on the activities individually or in small groups.

Lesson 14: Were the Procedures Used in This Situation Fair?

Teaching Procedures

A. Introducing the Lesson

Ask students what procedures they think might be useful when gathering information and making decisions in a school setting.

Have students read "Purpose of Lesson" on p. 230 of the text.

B. Critical Thinking Exercise
Evaluating, Taking, and Defending Positions

During this lesson the class will role-play a moot court hearing on issues of procedural justice described in the text. Post the following roles on the board:

- attorneys for the school
- attorneys for the student
- judges

Have students read the critical thinking exercise, "Evaluating, Taking, and Defending Positions," on pp. 230-231. The reading selection, "The State Examination," describes the way the school administration gathered information and made decisions when they suspected Lilly Adams of cheating on the New York State Regents Examination. With the class review the directions for completing the exercise and the questions in the "What do you think?" section on pp. 231-232. Also have students read "Procedures for a Moot Court Hearing" on p. 232 of the text. Review the procedures for participating in the activity with the class. For detailed instructions on conducting a moot court hearing, refer to p. 17 of this guide.

Assign students to the roles you have posted on the board. Distribute a copy to each student of the "Intellectual Tool Chart for Issues of Procedural Justice" on p. 229 of the student text. Allow adequate time for students to evaluate and develop positions on the issues presented in this case before conducting the moot court hearing. If you have invited a community resource person to the class, have the person work with students to evaluate this situation and to develop their positions on the issues. Ask your resource person to join the panel of judges for the presentation phase of the activity. The resource person should participate in the concluding discussion of this exercise and understand the intellectual tools.

C. Concluding the Lesson

Conclude the lesson by having the panel of judges share their decision with the class. Ask the judges to explain the reasoning that supports their decision.

Record their responses on the board. Ask the class to evaluate the decision in terms of the goals of procedural justice:

- Does the decision increase the chances of discovering the necessary information for making a wise and fair decision?
- Does it ensure the wise and fair use of the information in making decisions?
- Does it protect important values and interests?
- How were the intellectual tools useful in evaluating and developing positions on this issue?

Have students re-read "Purpose of Lesson" on p. 230 of the text. Ask them to describe the extent to which they achieved the objectives of the lesson.

Using the Lesson

The activities suggested in "Using the Lesson" on p. 232 of the text reinforce or extend what students have learned about intellectual tools used in dealing with issues of procedural justice. When working on the activities, encourage students to use the four steps they learned in this unit. Students may work individually or in small groups.

Lesson 15: Were the Procedures Used in This Administrative Hearing Fair?

Lesson Overview

Students are given a final exercise in applying the intellectual tools used in dealing with issues of procedural justice. The reading selection describes the procedures used to gather information and make decisions during a Commission on Civil Rights investigation into claims that people had been unfairly deprived of their right to vote. The activity of the lesson involves the class in role-playing a congressional hearing.

Lesson Objectives

At the conclusion of this lesson, students should be able to do the following:

- evaluate a situation dealing with issues of procedural justice
- take and defend positions in a situation dealing with issues of procedural justice using the intellectual tools

Preparation/Materials Required

Student text pp. 233-235

A copy for each student of the "Intellectual Tool Chart for Issues of Procedural Justice" on p. 229 of the student text

Optional: Invite a community resource person to the class such as an attorney or someone from a local civil rights agency

Teaching Procedures

A. Introducing the Lesson

While you post the "Terms to Know" on the board, have students read "Purpose of Lesson" on p. 233 of the text.

B. Critical Thinking Exercise
Evaluating, Taking, and Defending Positions

This critical thinking exercise involves the class in role-playing a congressional hearing. Before beginning the exercise, post the following roles on the board:

- Civil Rights Commission
- registrars
- N.A.A.C.P.
- registrars' union
- members of Congress

Have the class read the critical thinking exercise, "Evaluating, Taking, and Defending Positions," on pp. 233-234 of the student text. The reading selection, "The Civil Rights Commission," describes an investigation into claims that people had been denied their right to vote in violation of United States **civil rights** laws. With the class review the directions for completing the exercise and the questions in the "What do you think?" section on p. 234. Also have students read "Procedures for a Congressional Hearing" on p. 235 of the text. Review the roles and procedures for participating in the activity with the class. For detailed instructions on conducting a simulated congressional hearing, refer to p. 12 of this guide.

Assign students to the roles you have posted on the board. Distribute a copy to each student of the "Intellectual Tool Chart for Issues of Procedural Justice" on p. 229 of the student text. Allow adequate time for students to evaluate and develop positions on the issues presented in this case before conducting the hearing. If you have invited a community resource person to the class, have him or her work with the students to evaluate this situation and to develop their positions on the issues. Ask the resource person to join the members of Congress for the presentation phase of the activity. The resource person should participate in the concluding discussion of this exercise.

C. Concluding the Lesson

Conclude the lesson by having the members of Congress share their decision with the class. Ask the members of Congress to explain the reasoning that supports their decision. Record their responses on the board. Ask the class to evaluate the decision in terms of the goals of procedural justice:

- How were the intellectual tools useful in evaluating and developing positions on this issue?

- Does the decision increase the chances of discovering the necessary information for making a wise and fair decision?

- Does it ensure the wise and fair use of the information in making decisions?

- Does it protect important values and interests?

Have students re-read "Purpose of Lesson" on p. 233 of the text. Ask them to describe the extent to which they have achieved the objectives of the lesson.

Using the Lesson

The activities suggested in "Using the Lesson" on p. 235 of the text reinforce or extend what students have learned about intellectual tools used in dealing with issues of procedural justice. When working on the activities, encourage students to use the four steps they learned in this unit. Students may work individually or in small groups.

Concluding Exercise

Teaching Procedures

Have the class work in groups of three to four students. Ask students to read "What Issues of Justice Does This Situation Raise?" on p. 236 of the student text. Review the questions in the "What do you think?" section with the class. You may want to distribute to students a copy of each set of intellectual tools they learned while studying this curriculum. Allow adequate time for students to evaluate and to develop positions on how to fairly and properly respond to the issues raised in this situation. Have the students share their responses with the class.

To conclude the lesson, discuss their responses to the questions in the "What do you think?" section on p. 236.

This lesson concludes the study of Unit Four, "What Is Procedural Justice?" If students are keeping a journal, have them write a summary in their journals of what they have learned about using intellectual tools to develop and take positions on issues of procedural justice.

Concluding the Justice Curriculum

This concludes the study of the Justice curriculum. It will be valuable to both you and your students to reflect on and evaluate the total experience with this section of *Foundations of Democracy*, including the content and the instruction methods. Distribute to each student a copy of "Reflecting on Your Experience" on p. 28 of this guide. Remind students that they should not only reflect on and evaluate their experiences, but also those of the class. Have students share their responses with the class.

NOTES

NOTES

NOTES

NOTES